Contemporary South Africa

Contemporary States and Societies

This new series provides lively and accessible introductions to key countries and regions of the world, conceived and designed to meet the needs of today's students. The authors are all experts with specialist knowledge of the country or region concerned and have been chosen also for their ability to communicate clearly to a non-specialist readership. Each text has been specially commissioned for the series and is structured according to a common format.

Published

Contemporary Russia
EDWIN BACON with MATTHEW WYMAN
Contemporary South Africa
ANTHONY BUTLER
Contemporary America (2nd edition)
RUSSELL DUNCAN and JOSEPH GODDARD
Contemporary China
ALAN HUNTER and JOHN SEXTON
Contemporary Japan (2nd edition)
DUNCAN McCARGO
Contemporary Britain
JOHN McCORMICK
Contemporary Latin America
RONALDO MUNCK

Forthcoming

Contemporary India
KATHARINE ADENEY and ROBERT WYATT
Contemporary France
HELEN DRAKE
Contemporary Europe
B. GUY PETERS

Also planned

Contemporary Asia
Contemporary Germany
Contemporary Italy
Contemporary Spain

Contemporary
South Africa

Anthony Butler

palgrave
macmillan

First published 2004 by
PALGRAVE MACMILLAN
Houndmills, Basingstoke, Hampshire RG21 6XS and
175 Fifth Avenue, New York, N.Y. 10010
Companies and representatives throughout the world

PALGRAVE MACMILLAN is the global academic imprint of the Palgrave Macmillan division of St. Martin's Press, LLC and of Palgrave Macmillan Ltd. Macmillan® is a registered trademark in the United States, United Kingdom and other countries. Palgrave is a registered trademark in the European Union and other countries.

ISBN-13: 978–0–333–71518–5 hardback
ISBN-10: 0–333–71518–7   hardback
ISBN-13: 978–0–333–71519–2 paperback
ISBN-10: 0–333–71519–5   paperback

This book is printed on paper suitable for recycling and made from fully managed and sustained forest sources. Logging, pulping and manufacturing processes are expected to conform to the environmental regulations of the country of origin.

A catalogue record for this book is available from the British Library.

Library of Congress Cataloging-in-Publication Data
Bulter, Anthony, 1964–
        Contemporary South Africa / Anthony Butler.
             p. cm.
        Includes bibliographical references and index.
        ISBN 0–333–71518–7 (hbk.) ISBN 0–333–71519–5 (pbk.)
            1. South Africa – Politics and government – 1994– 2. South
    Africa – Economic conditions 1991 3. South Africa – Social
    conditions – 1994– I. Title.

DT1975.B87 2004
968.06'6—dc22   2003059564

10 9 8 7 6 5 4
13 12 11 10 09 08 07

Printed and bound in Great Britain by
Creative Print & Design (Wales), Ebbw Vale

For Julia and Anna

Contents

List of Tables, Figure, Maps and Boxes

x

Preface

Late twentieth century South Africa was notorious for apartheid, a system of legally institutionalized racial and ethnic segregation. Apartheid was organized around the enforced classification of a historically complex and diverse South African population as White, Native (later Bantu and then black), Indian, and coloured. These terms have been contested politically by many of those to whom they have been applied. Their use entrenches assumptions about racial difference that have no scientific validity. In this book, where racial terminology is of necessity used, the term 'African' refers to those officially classified as Native or black under apartheid. 'Black' refers more widely to all those not classified as White – that is to all those who were categorized as black, Indian, and coloured. I capitalise such terms throughout in order to emphazise their problematic nature.

This book attempts to reduce the complex and fast-changing reality of contemporary South Africa to a manageable text. I hope readers will forgive inevitable omissions and oversimplifications. In line with the series style, references have been kept to a minimum. Guides at the end of the book, however, direct interested readers towards a diversity of published and Internet sources of information and analysis on South Africa.

Colin Bundy, Anne Jellema, Samson Muradzikwa, HK Walker, and an anonymous reader offered generous advice on particular chapters. Cliff Butler's help was invaluable in the preparation of the final manuscript. Steven Kennedy has been an exemplary and patient editor. I am grateful to my colleagues at University of Cape Town, and especially to Bridgette Cloete, Robert Cameron, Thiven Reddy, Annette Seegers, Bob Mattes, Robert Schrire, Jeremy Seekings, Mary Simons, and Andre du Toit, for making the Department of Political Studies so pleasant and stimulating an environment in which to work.

Parts of Chapter 6 first appeared in volume 38 of *Government and Opposition*.

ANTHONY BUTLER
Cape Town
1 May 2003

Map 0.1   South Africa today

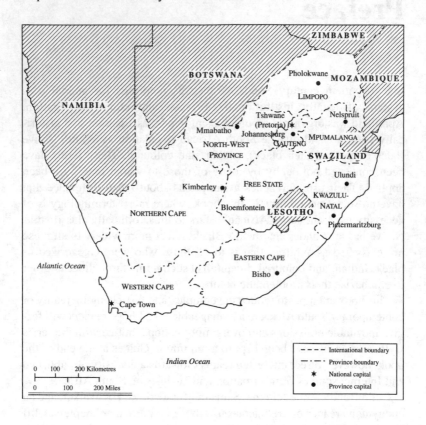

NAMIBIA

BOTSWANA

ZIMBABWE

Pholokwane

MOZAMBIQUE

LIMPOPO

Nelspruit

Mmabatho

Tshwane
(Pretoria)

Johannesburg

NORTH-WEST
PROVINCE

GAUTENG

MPUMALANGA

SWAZILAND

Ulundi

Kimberley

FREE STATE

KWAZULU-
NATAL

Bloemfontein

LESOTHO

Pietermaritzburg

NORTHERN CAPE

Atlantic Ocean

EASTERN CAPE

Bisho

WESTERN CAPE

Cape Town

Indian Ocean

| 0 | 100 | 200 Kilometres |
| 0 | 100 | 200 Miles |

- - - - International boundary
- · - · - Province boundary
*   National capital
●   Province capital

Introduction

South Africa's twentieth-century history was dominated by racial segregation and 'apartheid' – the systematic and institutionalized oppression of the county's non-White population. A decade after the country's first non-racial election in 1994 brought the African National Congress (ANC) to power, this history of division still profoundly influences the politics of the 'new' South Africa, and observers' predictions about the country's future. Pessimists view its political destiny through the lens of African decline, seeing the carefully managed 'transition to democracy' as just one more step along the road to the civil war, ethnic division, and one-party rule that has characterized so much of post-colonial Africa. Well-wishers see the new South Africa through quite different eyes, as a 'rainbow nation' unshackled by the 'miracle' of transition from the economic and social chains of apartheid. Many of the supporters of the ANC even see the liberation movement as the glorious locomotive of African renaissance, pulling the continent into the African century.

The presidency of Nelson Mandela, from 1994 to 1999, helped to calm those who feared that the future promised only tribalism, ungovernability, and civil war. For the anxious White minority, and for foreigners, new stereotypes of the 'patient masses' supplanted their once lurid fantasies of an ungovernable and radical African youth. The ANC's qualified alliances with the Afrikaner establishment and with F W de Klerk's National Party – the Dutch-descended instigators of apartheid – proved to be luxuries as the new government discovered it could govern without such partners.

The turbulent politics of opposition to apartheid quietly faded away. The urban poor returned to the business of survival. Wider educational and economic opportunities, and affirmative action within public and private sectors, helped the wealthiest fifth of Black South Africans to achieve substantial personal gains, and created a sizeable Black middle class for the first time. The economy did not boom in the 1990s, but neither did it collapse in a frenzy of populist redistribution, as some critics had feared. Indeed, an 'independent' central bank, conservative fiscal policy, revolutionized revenue collection, and an energetic finance ministry tamed inflation and banished a feared structural deficit. Rituals of reconciliation and restitution at the same time created the appearance of a society determined to put its past firmly behind it.

1

However, while the doom-mongers' worst fears had not been realized by 1999, Mandela's magic was little consolation for the poor. Employment creation over the ANC's first term remained far below the levels required to absorb an expanding working age population, and worker retrenchments spread vulnerability to multiple dependants. Poverty became even more deeply entrenched for the poorest quarter of South Africans, with dismaying indicators of rural child mortality, quality of life, and life expectancy. The extension of public services to the population as a whole, moreover, progressed very unevenly. While the government set out attractive sectoral policy frameworks, and came close to hitting tough delivery targets in house building, electrification, water supply, and health, critics complained with increasing urgency that ordinary citizens were experiencing insufficient improvement in their living standards. By 1999, according to a major household survey, 70 per cent of South Africans lived in a 'formal dwelling', up from two-thirds in 1995; but the proportion living in informal housing (such as shacks) had increased by half to over 12 per cent. Households with communal or individual access to clean water rose from 79 to just 83 per cent. A vast and expensive electrification programme spread electric lighting to almost three quarters of dwellings, while rendering only dangerous, polluting, and health-destroying household energy practices affordable, and failing to service nascent businesses (Statistics South Africa 2001).

Mandela left office in 1999 extraordinarily popular, but his presidency was nevertheless widely considered to have failed the test of 'delivery'. The arrival of his reputedly technocratic successor, after an active term as deputy president, was for this reason greeted with excitement. President Thabo Mbeki has not altogether disappointed these hopes. In his first three years he overhauled the national policy making machinery, clustered government departments to improve the co-ordination of policy, and started to remake municipalities into the developmental agents of the state. At the same time, he has strengthened the hand of the formidable Treasury, contained the growth of public debt, and built upon the personnel and policy strengths of Mandela's government. Mbeki's consistent external strategy has created new alliances within and beyond Africa and broken down Pretoria's long-standing isolation on the continent.

If it hit the ground running, however, Mbeki's administration had slowed markedly by the end of 2000. While citizens were sympathetic towards the government's difficulties in extending public services, the lack of employment opportunities, and persistently high levels of crime were matters of profound and growing dissatisfaction for South Africans of all classes. In this unpromising context, a stream of scandals and challenges buffeted the government in 2001. A major arms procurement package was hit by accusations of naivety, cost escalation, and high-level corruption. Inaction and confusion over the country's HIV/AIDS epidemic prompted protest and legal challenge, while the deepening crisis in neighbouring Zimbabwe became a source of growing domestic contention. Division over economic policy within the 'tripartite alliance' between the ANC, the South African Communist Party (SACP), and the Congress of South African Trade Unions (COSATU) burst into the open in late 2001. Public vitriol culminated in an anti-privatization strike, timed acutely by COSATU to embarrass the government in the midst of an international racism conference. The year ended with a major depreciation of the Rand. These many problems, however, were less cause for concern in themselves, than for the erosion of fragile democratic institutions they precipitated, and for the crisis of mutual incomprehension they exposed between critics and supporters of the government.

South Africa entered the new millennium a democracy with the potential to become a catalyst for regional recovery. Yet, for many, its economic and political prospects hang in the balance. Critics ask whether an ANC-dominated executive will eventually collide with the judiciary, damaging political institutions and undermining constitutional supremacy. They worry that negative perceptions will precipitate capital and skills flight, and that corruption may cross unknown thresholds to become a normal part of bureaucratic and economic interaction. Above all, perhaps, they wonder if the HIV/AIDS epidemic will lead to an economic slump or create a crisis of governance and governability.

The aim of this book is to provide a sophisticated introduction to modern South Africa that will clarify the key issues that lie behind answers to such questions. The first chapter explores the history of this unique country, and sets out the context within which current political and developmental challenges must be understood. Chapter 2 surveys the people of South Africa and their land, exploring the diversity of what Nobel Laureate Desmond Tutu famously called the 'rainbow nation'. The following two chapters look more deeply into the economic and social structures of the country. Chapter 3 details the political economy of the post-apartheid state, the organization and key sectors of the economy and the overall framework for economic policy. Chapter 4 investigates the structure of society, and explores causes of, and potential remedies for, the poverty and inequality that continue to blight national life. Chapters 5 and 6 turn to governing structures and to South Africa's lively politics, exploring how political institutions function under the new constitution, the nature and quality of political participation, the party system, and the longer-term prospects of democracy. Chapter 7 turns to cultural life and to the issues and ideas that animate intellectual interaction. Chapter 8 explores South Africa's external context, as a new force in African politics and a campaigner for continental renaissance. The final chapter appraises the ANC's performance to date, and looks ahead to assess South Africa's prospects across the rest of the twenty-first century.

1
Historical Context

South Africa is both a new democracy and a developing country. Her people are attempting a difficult experiment in political transformation while managing the economic and social strains that come with poverty, urbanization and economic development. Like the inhabitants of other developing countries, most South Africans must wage bitter struggles for access to scarce resources in a highly unequal society bequeathed by history.

Yet South Africans often consider themselves to be a special people. Their uniqueness, they believe, derives from their particular history of colonization, racial segregation, and triumphal democratization. At the heart of that exceptional history lies 'apartheid' – literally 'apartness' or separation. The legacies of segregation and apartheid, together with irreconcilable differences over their significance, continue to obstruct efforts to create a sustainable national identity and a coherent and inclusive social order.

South Africa before 1870

South Africa's unique history was decisively shaped by the discovery of diamonds and then gold from 1870, and then by the responses its imperial power, Britain, to the opportunities and threats these finds presented. Yet, if modern South African history begins with the 'minerals revolutions', the ramifications of these discoveries cannot be understood without first comprehending the complex balance of forces that in the 1870s characterized the area that is today South Africa. Four great historical stories – of the Khoisan peoples, African pastoralists and farmers, 'Boer' European-descended settlers, and British imperialists – are represented in any political map of the 1870s (see Map 1.1).

The least widely known of these histories concerns the subjugation of the earliest inhabitants of what is today South Africa. These hunting and herding societies, known today as Khoikhoi and San, or collectively Khoisan, had been present in the west and northwest since around 1000 BC.

Map 1.1   South Africa c. 1870

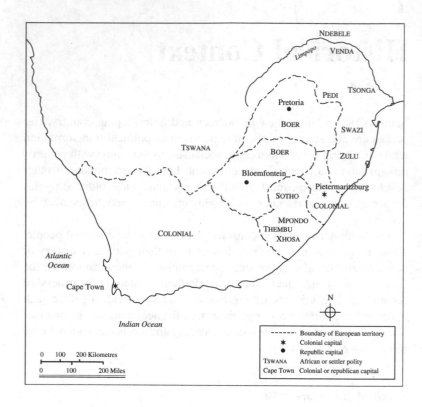

They fared particularly badly during the early period of European settlement – during Dutch East India Company rule from the mid-seventeenth century – with the settlers (and the diseases they brought with them) very rapidly subjugating them in the Cape.

In 1870, within the borders of the yet-to-be created South Africa, three more resilient modes of society, the actors in our three remaining great histories, were engaged in increasingly harsh competition for resources, but with none achieving predominance. The first and most important of these were Bantu-speaking African peoples – such as those who in the colonial period became known as the Xhosa or Zulu. Their resilience in the face of European settlement is evident in the widespread distribution of African polities after 200 years of colonial intrusion.

African political kingdoms had been expanding into what is today South Africa from around the third century AD. These dynamic African polities had spread by means of a 'migratory drift' or gradual territorial expansion almost to the west of South Africa by the time of European settlement. By the end of the eighteenth century, their population was reaching the limits of the potential of the South African land mass. The economies and social organization of these African societies were centred upon livestock. The effective political units of African pastoralism and farming were hereditary chiefdoms, varying in size from less than 1000 members to over 50 000. Chiefdoms were not closed entities, but rather included people of different descent groups, migrants from poor regions and arrivals who had broken away from other chiefdoms. These were not 'tribes', as Thompson (1990: 11) stresses: 'The Western concept of tribalism, which is usually taken to refer to closed populations reproducing fixed cultural characteristics, is not applicable to [these] African farmers.' Rather than closed entities with unique unchanging cultures, he observes, such societies were fluid and politically affiliative in composition. 'People interacted, co-operating and copulating as well as competing and combating, exchanging ideas and practices as well as rejecting them.'

The third extraordinary history concerns the 'Boers' (meaning farmers), primarily descended from the Dutch-speaking colonists of the Cape from the early seventeenth century, whose original function had been to supply passing ships of the Dutch East India Company. Initially a fuelling and provisioning station for the ships of the company, the Cape eventually became the springboard for settlers' dynamic if uncertain expansion. The experience of these Boer societies was in many respects similar to that of their African contemporaries. Their expansion north and east into the areas occupied by African polities began in the late eighteenth century. Boer settlers achieved advances through a combination of factors: exploitation of divisions in African society, (uneven) co-operation between Whites, the technological superiority of firearms, and the ability to store wealth in a more sophisticated economic system.

New opportunities for Boers were then unexpectedly created by a major transformation in African societies. As a result of a series of devastating conflicts, centring on the region between the mountain escarpment and the Indian Ocean, and driven by a centralization of the Zulu kingdom, there was a great dislocation of African farmers. The reasons for this upheaval are contested. Fresh territory for exploitation had become exhausted, and competition for land and water supplies grew. Severe droughts in the early nineteenth century triggered a process of concentration of power, and led to the emergence of a new scale of standing armies. The series of major conflicts that ensued dislocated the region's economies, and displaced great numbers of refugees. Some historians argue that foreign trade caused or contributed to Zulu state centralization, with competition to control trade routes spurring militarization. Whatever the dynamics of dislocation, the resulting turmoil presented White settlers with an unprecedented opportunity to colonize seemingly 'empty' and unclaimed land.

Meanwhile, the Cape colony became inhospitable to Boers. Britain, which had taken direct control over the Cape in 1795 to pre-empt French intervention, was introducing cultural and legal changes which damaged their interests and threatened to curtail their hitherto untrammelled power over their labourers. The influence of the ideals of the French Revolution, and evangelical anti-slavery campaigns in England, threatened Boers' customary practices of quasi-slavery. For them, migration to the immediate east was blocked by Xhosa chiefdoms which, in frontier wars, had demonstrated political and military resilience. Many Boers therefore embarked upon what came to be celebrated, a century later, as the 'Great Trek'. In reality this was a series of episodic migrations in the late 1830s totalling about 12 000 persons, half of whom were Khoi servants and former slaves. These 'Trekkers' battled sporadically with African polities, settling firstly in Natal and then (after British annexation of Natal) in the 'highveld' to the north. They secured effective independence from the British since a waning of abolitionist sentiment left London less well disposed to protect African against Trekker. The Boers remained poor and vulnerable, and in quite incomplete control of the territory over which they had claimed the right to rule. But, by 1870, they had established a tenuous presence across great tracts of the African interior.

The final narrative is that of the imperial power, Britain, which increasingly but unevenly predominated over the economy and politics of the coastal regions. These far less numerous British settlers, who complete our survey of pre-1870s polities, were backed by the immense but largely unexercised power of a great empire. London behaved in a characteristically calculating manner, expending few resources on what it viewed as a backwater. The Cape Colony was consolidated as a British possession after 1806 only because of its strategic location on trading routes to India. 'Like the Dutch before them', Thompson (1990: 53) remarks, 'the British had no vital material interest in South Africa beyond the peninsula. But appended to that strategic prize was a complex,

violent, and largely anarchic society, scattered over a vast hinterland.'
The limited importance London attached to South Africa was reflected
in the small proportion of British overseas capital attracted to it, modest
British immigration by comparison with other colonies, and a paucity of
manpower and resources. By 1870, the United States had 32 million
inhabitants of European origin or descent, and 53 000 miles of railways;
Southern Africa as a whole possessed 250 000 White people and around
70 miles of railways. The total value of imports was only £3 million per
annum, and exports were even less (Thompson 1990: 53, 108). The
biggest town contained only 50 000 inhabitants.

The 'turbulent hinterland' continued to command little attention
through the early and mid-nineteenth century. In the face of potential
alliances between Sotho and 'Trekker' (migrant Boer), the British were
willing to concede Boer independence in the South African Republic
(later Transvaal) in 1852. Further Sotho resistance led to a truce between
Europeans and to colonial withdrawal (Worden 1994: 16). While the
mid-nineteenth century was a time of limited British migration, the 1820
Conservative government, eager to placate domestic critics, funded the
migration of 4000 settlers from the British Isles to the eastern Cape agricultural belt. Rapidly adopting trading and commercial occupations,
these migrants remained culturally distinct from Afrikaner settlers, creating a nascent antagonism within the White population that went on to
deepen and persists today.

'Reform' influences in Britain were not decisive in dividing Whites.
Participation in the slave trade was outlawed in 1807 (depriving Cape
farmers of easy labour access), and from 1823 minimum standards of
food, clothing and maximum working hours and punishments were
patchily enforced in a spillover from a Caribbean tax on slavery. Further
legislation secured the legal position of the Khoi-Khoi and former
slaves, although it could not remove their poverty and economic
dependence. As Thompson (1990: 65) puts it, 'the reforms were the
reforms of freedom, but the facts were still the facts of exploitation'. The
tide of philanthropy, in any event, ebbed in Britain by the mid-nineteenth
century, and British settlers were increasingly faced with the same conditions as Afrikaners: insecure frontiersmen fighting against Africans for
land legally granted to them without the consent of its customary inhabitants. They brought with them the scientistic racism of mid-Victorian
Britain, and adapted it adroitly to their new circumstances.

A seeming retreat of British colonial power in the mid-nineteenth
century was belied by the establishment of considerable colonial

economic influence by the 1850s. While Afrikaners lay beyond the reach of systematic imperial constraint, the colonial heartland was increasingly incorporated into the Empire. Trade was centred on the Cape, and migrant labour had been drawn to the colony from the 1840s. Where Cape interests were threatened, intervention by the imperial power was rapid and effective. Moreover, the very fact of possession brought with it an inescapable if unwanted responsibility to provide a modicum of law and order in the frontier zone. These pressures, mediated through military, evangelical and commercial interests, resulted in a continuous stream of (to Boers) unwanted interventions by the British authorities.

Many twentieth-century histories of South Africa penned by Europeans wrongly viewed the African societies of 1870 as static 'tribes' impacted by dynamic settlers. There was little sign among African societies of the social disintegration that had affected the indigenous peoples of many other colonies. Change within these robust polities was primarily driven by domestic rather than colonial factors, accelerating in the early nineteenth century with the rise of the Zulu kingdom (Beinart 1994: 16). Africans jostled with vulnerable Afrikaners and isolated colonialists who could command few of the resources of the imperial power. Many Africans, moreover, were using the economic opportunities presented by settlement and trade to their advantage (Bundy 1988).

All of Southern Africa's relatively small 1870s quasi-states were multi-ethnic and multi-lingual. Most of them lacked the bases of political and cultural unity, and limited political self-consciousness was the rule. The history of the polities in the 1870s could never be told as an attempt to master collective destiny. Political leaders were attempting to survive in unforgiving circumstances, and the part-mythical histories through which they justified their claims to rule were themselves ever-changing.

The Creation of the State, 1870–1910

Post-1870 South Africa was marked by a new speed and magnitude of social change and the populations of the area were driven by a common series of impersonal forces. The roots of this upheaval lay in discoveries of diamonds and gold, and in the responses of the British colonial power to these discoveries. Four massive processes marked the transformation

Box 1.1   Key dates in South African history

c. 1000 BC	Khoikhoi herders living in South Africa
c. 300 AD	Bantu-speaking farmers move into South Africa
1652	Dutch East India Company establishes Cape Town settlement
1806	Britain establishes control over Cape Colony
1816–28	Centralized Zulu kingdom conquers neighbours
1834	Slave emancipation
1835–40	Afrikaner 'Great Trek' to interior
1867	First diamonds discovered
1877	Britain annexes Transvaal
1878–79	British defeat Tswana, Zulu, Pedi, commence Transkei annexation
1886	Gold mining begins on the Witwatersrand
1899–1902	British defeat Afrikaners in South African ('Boer') War
1910	Union of South Africa established
1912	South African Native National Congress (later ANC) formed
1914–19	Participation in the First World War as part of British empire
1923	*Natives (Urban Areas) Act* formalizes urban segregation
1939–45	Contested participation alongside Allies in the Second World War
1948	National Party elected on 'apartheid' slogan
1950	*Group Areas* and *Population Registration* Acts
1960	Police kill 67 demonstrators at Sharpeville
1961	South Africa becomes a Republic
1964	Nelson Mandela and other opposition leaders imprisoned for life
1969	Foundation of South African Students' Organisation under Steve Biko
1975–76	Mozambique and Angola become independent
1976–77	Revolt in Soweto followed by national unrest
1976–81	'Independence' conferred upon four of the Bantustans
1980	Zimbabwe independent
1985	Foundation of ANC-aligned union federation COSATU
1986	Pass laws repealed
1989	F W de Klerk becomes President
1990	Opposition parties unbanned; Mandela and others released
1991	Repeal of apartheid legislation; formal negotiations begin at CODESA
1994	ANC wins first non-racial election: Mandela becomes president
1999	ANC wins second national election: Thabo Mbeki is president
2000–	HIV/AIDS epidemic

of South Africa over this period: war, unification, economic development, and the forging of a migrant working class.

Diamonds were discovered in 1867, attracting foreign investment, initiating modern capitalism in South Africa, and creating unprecedented demand for labour. By 1871, 75 000 people had flocked to the diamond fields, and development created labour shortages not just in the mines, but also on the farms, in new industries, on the railways and in public works. Diamonds were soon overtaken by gold, discovered in 1886 on the Witwatersrand ('white waters reef') and soon to transform the entire southern African region. While the metal ore was of low quality and difficult to extract, potential gold wealth was vast, and the metal was central to the liquidity and stability of the then gold-based international economy. Its effective and immediate exploitation was for these reasons a British strategic imperative. In order to accomplish this, the imperial power required a massive input of cheap domestic and skilled foreign labour, together with the infrastructure, regulation, and stability that only a complex and unified modern state could provide.

The demands for stability and for labour led the imperial power to break the resistance of African polities through military force. Then, at great cost, they subdued the Afrikaners in the South African or Boer War of 1899–1902. Unification was the ultimate goal of war. Far from merely representing a legalistic or constitutional device, unification was a comprehensive process of state creation. British power built the machinery of state control through which it could enforce contracts, secure transport links, regulate labour and business, and ensure strategic security across the area of contemporary South Africa as a whole. By so doing it ensured that the mineral wealth of South Africa could be exploited safely by British-based conglomerates.

Economic development in the new urban areas, the third key process of change, was signalled by the extraordinary growth of Johannesburg and the Witwatersrand region, and by the wholesale transformation of the economic geography of South Africa. Johannesburg did not exist in 1880. By 1911 it contained 240 000 inhabitants, and the Witwatersrand as a whole held twice that number. Cape Town, by contrast, contained less than 200 000 people and was to become thereafter something of an economic backwater. The new urban areas were a maelstrom of diversity, encompassing low-waged miners and highly paid immigrants, and a plethora of races and classes. The state carefully managed the influx of African labour, using already embedded practices and ideologies. Britain's High Commissioner Milner viewed native reserves, urban 'influx' control, and the manipulation of chiefs as necessary instruments to keep Africans in check in the colonial economy. Social Darwinism helped justify segregationist policies, and further ideological support was provided by new racial doctrines from the United States.

The fourth major process of change in South Africa lay in part beyond the towns. South Africa developed a system of 'migrant labour' that was to mark its later twentieth-century history – the cyclical and often annual movement of able-bodied young African labourers into and out of the core urban economy. Migrant labour in South Africa began on the sugar fields of Natal which depended upon labourers from Mozambique. Later cyclical migrancy became a generalized domestic and sub-continental cheap labour system, feeding the country's mining, commercial, and agricultural sectors. Ultimately it became the backbone of the industrial and commercial systems of apartheid as a whole. The mine owners' preference for such migrant labour, primarily because it was cheap, initially coincided with some Africans' own interests. Young male urban labourers – nine out of every ten of the 1910 Black population of Johannesburg was male – provided money for chiefs and for fathers. Only gradually (and in large measure through systematic and deliberate government action) did money become necessary for survival in rural South Africa, and migrant labour correspondingly become a necessity for survival. By the 1920s, 30–40 per cent of active men in rural areas were away at work at any given time.

While White Supremacy and segregation predated and shaped this period of transformation, the impersonal forces of market, imperial power, and capital were the primary driving agents of change. The 1910 *Act of Union* formalized the new state's existence and cemented its political structures. It served, moreover, to entrench the privileged interests of Whites by means of a racialized political machinery. Whites secured a virtual monopoly of electoral power, with a property franchise retained in the Cape colony alone. This period of South African history laid the economic, political, and institutional foundations of segregation and apartheid.

Segregation and Early Apartheid: 1910–60

The decade after 1910 saw continued English dominance and deepening racial segregation under the auspices of a political alliance between Afrikaner agriculture, White mine owners, and those dependent on them (Terreblanche and Nattrass 1990). During post-unification reconstruction, labour supply remained at the heart of government policy. Native reserves, 'influx controls', and compliant 'traditional authorities', became reliable policy instruments for a state supporting mining and agricultural capital. The African population was increasingly pervasively regulated where it remained on the land, and further forged into a working class through the migrant labour system.

The *Natives Land Act* of 1913 allocated 87 per cent of land to Whites and moved to prohibit native land purchase and non-labour based tenancies. The 1923 *Urban Areas Act* created legal tools to entrench further the practices of segregation and 'influx control' (the coercive management of migration to work in the cities). Initially a partly discretionary process through which cash income supplemented rural economic activity, influx control eventually became unavoidable as taxes, dispossession, and population growth squeezed rural populations. The Chamber of Mines used chiefs, traders, and criminals to recruit young, male workers, and from 1910 became increasingly cost-focused and geographically ambitious in recruitment. By 1920, a centralized labour migration system managed more than 200 000 workers, a number that was to grow in later years, reaching a peak of 430 000 migrants in 1961.

Open class conflict meanwhile intensified in White South Africa between 1907 and 1933, a period of economic nationalism and struggle between mining capital and White workers. The 1922 Rand Revolt, in which Afrikaans- and English-speaking Whites fought against capitalism but also against Blacks, was crushed only by considerable military firepower and at the cost of over 200 lives. The government of 1924, which combined Hertzog's National Party with the Labour Party, oversaw the foundations of an Afrikaner welfare state. The emergence of Afrikaner nationalism, itself a creature of social dislocation, served as a bridge across regional and class divides.

From 1933 to 1948, South Africa emerged from the depression into a second industrial revolution. On the back of a rise in the gold price which followed the collapse of the Gold Standard, and further bolstered by increased demand for manufactured exports as the North prepared for global war, the economy grew rapidly with English interests spreading out from their heartland in the gold-mining economy. General economic affluence, fuelled by gold and the export boom, helped to fund government welfare and agricultural support programmes. The period also, however, saw the growth of D.F. Malan's 'purified' National Party, with dreams of more complete racial segregation. White unity, furthermore, was shattered over the issue of participation on the side of the Allies in the Second World War. After the 'fusion government' was formed in 1934, the breakaway National Party had managed to mobilize Afrikaners nationally by deploying cultural and educational organizations,

Afrikaner unions, and business groups. Farmers, civil servants, teachers, and poor Whites turned increasingly towards the Nationalists.

The mid- to late-1930s marked a first high point of segregation. Legislation passed in 1936 consolidated the native reserves and removed propertied Africans from the Cape voter roll. This was also a low point of Black resistance. The African National Congress, elitist, isolated from labour and radical protest since its foundation in 1913, continued on its ineffectual way. Indian and Coloured political movements organized around particularist or local concerns. Political resistance was largely expressed within churches and through widespread non-compliance with the law. Politics for Africans was a defensive process: the use of forms of traditional authority and religious belief to defend land rights and grazing, and to advance localized interests in urban situations.

The wartime economic bonanza of 1939–48 saw a relaxation of segregation and an inexorable urbanization. White and Black alike were drawn to the towns, but the change in Africans' situation was striking. Between 1936 and 1946, their numbers in urban areas grew from 139 000 to 390 000, and for the first time many of these were women. The presence of Africans in the urban economy was expressed politically in a number of ways. Black trade unions blossomed, higher-skilled jobs were opened to Africans, and colour bars in many sectors floated upwards. The formal structures of African politics – notably the ANC Youth League from 1944 – began to organize deliberately integrative protests to draw together the opponents of segregation. The South African Communist Party arranged anti-pass campaigns in 1943–44. Bus boycotts became a major instrument of protest, strikes escalated across the war years, and thereafter the turmoil continued into the peace as the younger generation of activists, led by Nelson Mandela and Oliver Tambo, galvanized the ANC into action, catalysing strikes and politically motivated land occupations on the Rand.

The year 1948 is a significant date in modern South African history: the year in which the Afrikaner 'National Party' won the first of many election victories under the slogan of 'apartheid'. The National Party (NP) was to remain in power until the first universal franchise election of 1994. Continuities between pre-war segregation and post-war 'apartheid', however, were far more striking than the discontinuities. Only in the 1960s, with the second phase of apartheid, did Afrikaner power exert itself to produce the unprecedented social deformation of high apartheid. Why, then, has 1948 so often been taken to be the key date in South African twentieth-century political history?

First, the general election of 1948 represented a decisive triumph for a new and non-conciliatory generation of Afrikaner politicians in the NP. This victory was a slender one and represented no massive swing in White (or even Afrikaner) sentiment. Defeated Prime Minister Jan Smuts lost much Afrikaner support because of 'swamping' fears associated with Black urbanization and the presence of Africans in jobs formerly reserved for (war-mobilized) Whites. Local issues made a major impact in Natal, where anti-Indian land restrictions played a central role. In the Transvaal and Orange Free State, doubts among farmers about labour supply and the intentions of the United Party (UP) led to a swing to Malan's National Party, despite the latter's Cape origins and core support. Four-tenths of Afrikaners voted for the UP, and the NP relied on the votes of 20 per cent of English speakers to achieve their overall 39 per cent (Beinart 1994: Chapter 5). Once again, fortune smiled on the NP. While the UP and Labour won 53 per cent between them, the NP secured narrow victories in more heavily weighted rural and peri-urban constituencies. The pivotal 1948 election victory was therefore fortuitous, turning on minority and protest voters. The changed electoral coalitions that secured long-term NP power came earlier and later. Afrikaner nationalism was already a cross-class and inter-regional force that could potentially unify labour and agriculture around the policy of segregation. Afrikaner control over the White electorate as a whole was still to be established.

The second reason for the predominance of 1948 as the key date in twentieth-century South African historical writing was a slogan: 'apartheid' (or apartness). The term first rose to prominence in the NP's electoral campaign of 1948 and became a common figure of speech across White South Africa in that year. The apartheid of 1948 was not, however, the apartheid of the 1960s. This would be to read history backwards. The slogan 'apartheid', along with the fears of Black urbanization and job competition to which it drew attention, was an important asset of the NP in its marginal minority win in 1948. Its power lay in its very ambiguity. NP supporters agreed that Africans should continue to be excluded from political power and that White supremacy should be maintained. Beyond this, however, apartheid provided a means of papering over great differences. Should Afrikaners strive for total segregation, with the replacement of African labour by White labour (by birth or migration), as many intellectuals, clerics, teachers argued? Or should businessmen and agriculturalists continue to have access to Black labour in a pragmatic and moderated form of segregation? Appealing to new voters, those demobilized from the military, and building cross-class and cross-regional support from a diverse electorate, the slogan 'apartheid' was an accidental success of political rhetoric.

A third reason for the significance attached to 1948 is a body of repugnant legislation enacted by the NP immediately after its first electoral victory. This legislation included the *Population Registration Act*, which enforced the classification of people into four strict racial categories: White, Coloured, Indian/Asiatic, and Native (later Bantu or African). This fourfold classification provided a basis for the systematic social and economic engineering of 'high apartheid' that was to come. In the first period of NP rule, however, the focus was on symbolically important aspects of life as much as upon the economics of the labour market. 'Mixed marriages' were prohibited in 1949, and in 1950 all sexual contact between Whites and other South Africans was prohibited in an *Immorality Act*. Residential segregation was another focus of legislative activity, with the *Group Areas Act* of 1950 applying residential segregation by race comprehensively across the country. The *Reservation of Separate Amenities Act* of 1953 segregated transport, cinemas, restaurants, and sporting facilities, and later acts enforced segregation in schools, colleges, and universities. Unlike much of the law that succeeded it, 'petty' apartheid legislation was not designed to reshape South Africa's structures of economic opportunity but was distinguished by its undisguised racial malevolence.

Three factors in combination – the electoral win of the NP, the significance that the term apartheid later accrued, and the repugnancy of early NP legislation – made 1948 a year of seemingly unprecedented importance. The myth of 1948 as a great break in South African history has been manifest in the notion that apartheid was a 'Grand Plan', unfolded by NP leaders in the 30 years following 1948. The idea of a grand plan became established because of its attractiveness to both liberals and Afrikaners. The former used the notion to condemn Afrikaners as fanatical imposers of a systematic oppression. The latter overemphasized their control over events and concealed the messy reality of oppression behind the moral perfectionism of a project. Scholars, however, have shown that NP policy represented a pragmatic continuation of pre-1948 government strategy – albeit an intensification of it – and a reactive series of responses by the party.

Not merely in the economic sphere, but more generally across the fields of social policy, apartheid in the 1950s represented a series of ad hoc attempts to resolve embedded problems. In urban areas, nationalists wanted to re-establish control over Black population growth, and embarked on a 'stabilization' strategy of squatter camp destruction, the 'purification' of

White areas, and township construction. In rural areas, the messy compromises of re-tribalization were formalized through the *Bantu Authorities Act* of 1951 into a distinct realm of African politics with an associated 'traditional' system of administration and authority (Bonner *et al.* 1993: 15–21).

As Deborah Posel (1991) has shown, the steady consolidation represented by the policies of the 1948 government's legislation does not imply a great degree of planning or control. Proponents of the NP's ability to plan systematically point to the government commissioned *Sauer Report* of 1947. This document gave substance to the slogan of apartheid while uniting the farmers of the Transvaal, Orange Free State, and the Cape, with White labour and the Afrikaner petty bourgeoisie. Posel demonstrates, however, that this report reproduced divergences within Afrikanerdom rather than settling them. The total segregationist aspirations of intellectuals and petty bourgeois Afrikaners were irreconcilable with the practical designs of prosperous Afrikaner industrialists and financiers. The effort to accommodate them led to an 'ambiguous combination of purist and "practical" recommendations', leaving the 1948 government without a 'compelling, unambiguous, and uncontested blueprint from which state policies could simply be read off' (Posel 1991: 60).

Not only was there no consistent plan, moreover, there were immediate and inescapable pressures upon NP leaders. Their policies had to satisfy not merely Afrikaner interests but also English capital and the largest opposition controlled local authorities. They also faced the threat of African resistance and the nagging danger of electoral desertion (Posel 1991: 6). They secured their position rapidly and skilfully, first by consolidating the electoral dominance of the NP by abolishing the 'Cape franchise' (which had provided some non-Whites with the vote) and rigging the Namibian constituency contribution. Second, the NP fostered a new moral climate among White electors as a whole. The blatant and systematic racism of 1950s legislation, combined with population classification, made possible the conception of quite distinct social lives being created for distinct racial and ethnic groups. Third, it sidelined English-speaking bureaucrats and advanced Afrikaners, in particular members of the secretive nationalist establishment group, the Broederbond. 'Bond' members became instruments of Afrikaner political dominance, by the mid-1950s occupying key positions in the heartlands of executive power. The Native Affairs Department (NAD), in particular, grew to be a state-within-a-state, within which the policies of the 1960s fomented.

State intervention was a defining theme of 1950s politics. The Nationalists, according to Bonner *et al.* (1993: 31), believed that 'most of the problems [the state] confronted in 1948 could be solved effectively by simply expanding the scope and intensity of state intervention on the social, political, and economic fronts'. Even where the NP appeared to be following a new and distinctively statist route, it seems very likely that a UP government would have followed very much the same one, since the structural problems facing the economy would have predisposed any government towards these policies. The Fagan Commission report of 1946 had recommended 'ideally voluntary' labour bureaux and identity documents in its prescriptions for the control of African urbanization (even while admitting that such population movements had to be tolerated). The UP put its name to Fagan's recommendations. Had the UP won that election, 'there is good reason to suppose that the shift into a more statist era would have happened anyway' (Bonner *et al.* 1993: 31).

The Rise and Fall of 'High Apartheid'

The governments of the 1950s were in certain respects unexceptional. White supremacy and the exclusion of Africans from participation in formal political activity were the norm in colonial Africa. Apartheid's second phase in the 1960s, by contrast, represented a qualitatively distinct period in South African history, bringing a change of direction rather than merely a cumulatively deepening segregation. Mass forced removals of 'incorrectly' located Black people, newly created homelands or Bantustans, and deliberate 're-tribalization', added up to a quite new scale of social engineering. The reach of the state increased, the policing system intensified, and distinct security and military apparatuses competed to dominate the South African state's executive core (see Chapter 8).

Segregationist doctrine was supplanted by the more dangerous notion 'separate development'. This involved the idea that Africans and others should reside, and enjoy citizenship rights, in distinct ethnic homelands. Whereas White supremacy and segregation had involved an explicit racial hierarchy in legislative and political practice, the NP from 1961 was committed to formal equality between groups understood in ethnic terms. The inspiration for these moves was in part the decolonization movements elsewhere in Africa, and especially the experiences of the former British protectorates of Botswana, Lesotho, and Swaziland, which many Afrikaner political leaders had earlier hoped to incorporate into South Africa in recognition that they were dependent on the Witwatersrand economy. If African nationalists could press for the independence of artificial and arbitrarily defined states, then why could not equally artificial states be granted 'independence' within South Africa itself? 'Separate development' was the key concept in this phase of apartheid. Africans' political rights were transferred ultimately into 10 Bantustans, and in 1970 homeland citizenship was forced upon all Africans. In the following decade, four of the homelands were nominally, and without international recognition, declared independent (see Map 1.2).

The doctrine of separate development implied that every South African must be assigned to an ethnic group, nation, or tribe, and that each of these must have its own site of self-government. Ethnic categories were enforced on a largely unwilling Black populace by means of comprehensive social engineering. Communities, and even families, were divided as the bureaucracy of apartheid categorized an entire people in accordance with rules of descent. Consequent population removals, simplified now by a clear classification by race and ethnic group, could adopt a stark brutality. Between 1960 and 1989, there were 3.5 million forced removals of people who were found to be of 'incorrect' ethnicity for their location.

The homelands never came close to acquiring economic self-sufficiency or political legitimacy. As a contribution to their viability, the South African government introduced incentives for business to locate on their borders. The major source of income, however, was always

Map 1.2   South Africa under apartheid

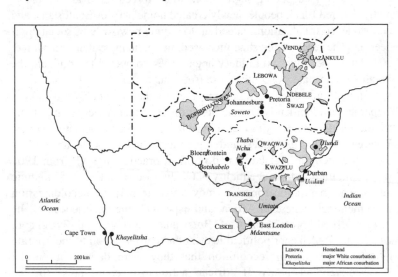

work in the core (now White) economy. Bantustans were justified primarily as political homes for ethnicities, bolstered by systematic 'retribalisation'. Ethnicity or tribalism was established as the principal foundation of homeland self-government, with ethnic affiliation designed to displace South African nationality as the proper basis of African political identification. The official ethnic divisions of 1960s South Africa had plainly been defined by European academics and missionaries who in earlier decades recorded what they took to be permanent 'tribal' languages and cultures. It transpires they were quite mistaken in doing so (see Box 1.2).

Under apartheid, created tribalism was given fresh impetus by a deliberate project of 're-tribalization'. New groups emerged that found tribalism and the homeland system to be in their interest: the political

---

Box 1.2   Three views of 'tribalism'

Tribalism has been understood in three ways. A crude 'essentialist' view of African ethnicity saw the warrior 'tribe' as a timeless community with a common essence in shared language, culture, and physical appearance, aspects passed from generation to generation. Such tribes were seen as inherently antagonistic and prone to bouts of warfare. A later 'instrumentalist' view saw the modern tribe as an instrument of colonial rule. Academics, missionaries, and colonial administrators 'invented' tribal practices, conjured pseudo-languages out of dialects, and persuaded a new African elite through missionary education to embrace these invented traditions. Overstretched colonial administrators used tribes to divide and rule, to maintain law and order, to collect taxes, and to extract labour. Contemporary scholars hold a third and more sophisticated 'constructivist' view, which recognizes that ethnicity could never simply be imposed or invented. Rather it had to be built out of the beliefs and experiences of Africans. Missionaries' teaching of written African languages, they concede, did create the linguistic preconditions for modern tribalism. Native administrators did find tribalist ideas useful in controlling those whom they wished to exploit. According to constructivists, however, local chiefs and currently predominant clans themselves created a-historical 'tribal' justifications for their power, in order to turn their temporary hegemony into permanent rule. The African teachers and intellectuals exposed to the colonizers' interpretations of African history in missionary schools themselves benefited from tribalism as interpreters of tradition for the colonizers and interpreters of colonial practice for 'traditional leaders'. Migrant labourers, for their part, were reliant for survival of networks on support in the hostels and squatter settlements, and discovered in place of origin and nuance of dialect the foundations for systems of mutual trust and support.

and bureaucratic elites of the Bantustans. Each Bantustan, destined for political independence, required separate political, judicial and executive institutions, together with a political elite (often drawn from existing 'traditional leaders') to exercise government. These 'homeland bureaucrats' were joined by a new homeland-based African business class which exploited the withdrawal of White traders and businessmen and took advantage of state investment subsidies.

While Africans' political rights were confined to the Bantustans, 'democratic' elections meanwhile furnished the NP with the legitimacy to entrench its rule. The Broederbond had by 1960 established itself in the heartland of the South African executive and oversaw an ambitious centralization of state powers. The local authorities that had obstructed influx control in the 1950s were easily circumvented by a 1960s central state that had acquired the machinery to run influx control virtually independently of them. African political resistance strengthened the hand of those arguing for new measures, and for the far-reaching revolution of separate development. It was individual acts of defiance of influx control, however, repeated by millions of workers, that made the system ultimately unsustainable. Between 1960 and 1970, while the African population in White urban areas fell by over 200 000, the population of the Bantustans grew by almost a million. The extreme overcrowding and impoverishment that resulted in the reserves, and the artificial reduction in available labour in the White urban areas, created a strong incentive for millions of workers to defy the system of influx control.

Explaining South Africa's 'Transition to Democracy'

How did this great structure of high apartheid crumble? What processes explain its demise? How was the 'miracle' of democratic transition negotiated between a racist regime and its 'terrorist' ANC opponent? Long-range international developments profoundly influenced the circumstances within which apartheid collapsed and a democratic settlement was ultimately negotiated. Economic nationalism became decreasingly viable in any country in the 1970s and 1980s as international financial movements and floating exchange rates defeated state defences. The importance of technology transfer and international collaboration for modern industry redoubled these pressures (Goodman and Pauly 1993). Theorists of economic deregulation eventually made inescapable a new neo-classical orthodoxy or 'Washington consensus' fundamentally at odds with the statist and anti-market foundations of apartheid. Domestically, the South African state had long faced a structural crisis. Influx control institutions, never very effective in operation, began to crumble, and urban Black populations to grow rapidly. The effects of South Africa's long-standing productive investment crisis in which investment barely replaced capital stock began to kick in sharply. The economic crisis of the Soviet bloc reduced the interest of the United States and other Western powers in client regimes such as South Africa, while Pretoria was gradually stripped of its buffer regimes to the north by the independence of Angola, Mozambique, Zimbabwe, and Namibia. Many simultaneous experiments in democracy around Southern Africa by the 1990s indicate how general were the pressures at work. The requirements of economic growth, inward investment, and international political legitimacy all pointed the same way. In South Africa, in combination with the stagnation of the economy, the collapse of labour control, and urbanization, these pressures made collaboration between the ANC and the NP government a very great likelihood rather than an unexpected miracle.

While this context pointed towards a negotiated transition, it required decades of organized political opposition to close down the NP's avenues for evasion and delay. The endgame of the fight against apartheid saw extended struggle between a militarised Afrikaner regime and a powerful mass protest movement – which included organized labour, students, schoolchildren, and community associations – that was able to exert continuous tactical pressure on the regime. Independent Black trade unions in the 1980s formed a formidable ANC-aligned Federation (later Congress) of South African Trade Unions (COSATU) that ultimately proved able to bring the economy to a standstill. Young people and students, after the watershed youth revolt that began in Soweto in 1976, were a relentless force for protest and change. Meanwhile ideological shifts among political and economic elites led to the progressive desertion of Afrikaner intellectuals and the development of contacts between the ANC in exile and South African business leaders. In the new President from 1989, F W de Klerk, the process of negotiation finally found an adroit and brave Afrikaner tactician (see Box 1.3).

The key parties' arrival at the negotiating table, albeit after a bruising and extended struggle, was ultimately unsurprising, and the prospects of a negotiated settlement would seem to have been bright. There were, after all, few identifiable ideological divides between the leaders of the NP and the ANC. Statist and South African nationalist, pragmatic about economic policy-making and public policy, each was evidently capable of compromise and sophisticated negotiation. Despite the diverse experiences of exile, imprisonment, and domestic struggle, ANC

Box 1.3   F W de Klerk

Frederik Willem de Klerk was born in Johannesburg on 18 March 1936, the son of Senator Jan de Klerk, later a minister in the South African government. De Klerk graduated in law from Potchefstroom University in 1958, and practised in Vereeniging in the Transvaal. A gifted analytical thinker, later offered a professorship of administrative law at Potchefstroom, de Klerk rose rapidly through the Transvaal National Party becoming member for Vereeniging by the early 1970s. In 1978, Prime Minister Vorster appointed him Minister of Posts and Telecommunications, the first of many ministerial portfolios. Under P. W. Botha, these included Mineral and Energy Affairs (1980–82), Internal Affairs (1982–85), and National Education and Planning (1984–89). As Minister of Education, he was a supporter of segregated universities but committed to increasing resources for non-Whites. A relative centrist in the Party who led moves in 1982 against the extreme right, he was not a natural reformer. In February 1989, de Klerk was elected leader of the NP and in September 1989 he became State President. In his first speech as party leader he called for negotiations about the country's future, and on 2 February 1990 he lifted the ban on the ANC and other banned political organizations, and announced the release of Nelson Mandela. While the ANC's achievement of non-racial democracy had not been de Klerk's goal, he was rewarded with a Nobel Peace Prize in 1993. After South Africa's first universal franchise democratic elections on 27 April 1994, de Klerk was appointed Executive Deputy President in South Africa's Government of National Unity (GNU), a post he held until the NP's June 1996 withdrawal from GNU.

---

members showed an almost pathological commitment to organizational accountability and cohesion. The NP had few serious doubts about the reliability and integrity of the military and (with some exceptions) the security apparatus. There was little likelihood of state disintegration or coup. Notwithstanding the violent conflict in Natal, moreover, there was little danger of a state destabilizing civil war. The means of state coercion remained too overwhelming to permit this possibility.

The negotiation process itself reflected the powerful forces for settlement, with continuity and predictability evident throughout. One insider's account discounts the significance of day-to-day political turmoil, pointing to the immense economic and international pressures that forced even hard-line NP leader Botha to begin contacts with the ANC in mid-1987 (Asmal 1995). FW de Klerk's relaxation of controls on political activity in 1989, after he wrested power from an ailing Botha, seems a natural corollary of this recognition. February 1990 ıbrought de Klerk's decisive legalization of opposition organizations, multiple unbannings of individuals, and selected releases of detainees. Soon after, exiles were allowed to return, and the State of Emergency was lifted. Concentrated and extensive negotiations embarked upon in 1991 ended at Christmas with a reasonably unproblematic statement of joint commitment to negotiation through a Convention for a Democratic South Africa. CODESA incorporated 18 political groups which each agreed to the goals of an 'undivided' South Africa, a bill of rights, a multi-party system, constitutional government, a separation of powers, civil liberties, and specified freedoms to be enjoyed by all citizens.

There were wrong turnings and reversals. The year 1992, in particular, was a year of stalemate. The CODESA working party on constitutional principles found itself unable to advance, especially on the size of majorities required to achieve control in the elected constitution-making body. However, even a temporary withdrawal of the ANC was not the dangerous risk that many analysts made it out to be. By March 1993, all 26 negotiating parties were back in public debate in the Multi-Party Negotiating Process. 'Consensus' was the basis upon which talks were based, although this rapidly became established as 'sufficient consensus'. As Johnston has remarked, ANC–NP negotiations were 'helped by the assumption on both sides that "sufficient consensus" meant consensus between themselves' (Johnston 1994: 722). As early as April 1993, technical committees were exploring solutions to problems in the fields of violence, discriminatory legislation, the media, the electoral commission, human rights, constitutional issues, and the Transitional Executive Council (or TEC) that was to take over executive functions in the run-up to the first non-racial election. By September, the Constitution of South Africa (known usually as the transitional or interim constitution) had been enacted and legislation on the conduct of a 'free and fair election' had been passed. The entire process had been enacted by existing institutions – as clear an indication as there could be of the degree of extraordinary control over events achieved by the key negotiating parties. Immense attention to detail was displayed in the drafting of the interim constitution: powers and rules were precisely specified and much of the document read like a detailed contract rather than a framework of general rules. The TEC – the alternative cabinet that was to be the ultimate executive authority in the run-up to the election – was regulated by detailed statutes. Other transitional arrangements were equally carefully defined, including a timeframe that required the final constitution be passed by May 1996, and to be formulated in accordance with 34 'Constitutional Principles' under the oversight of the Constitutional

Box 1.4   Nelson Mandela

Nelson Mandela was born at Qunu in the eastern Cape on 18 July 1918. His father was chief councillor to Thembuland's acting paramount chief and Mandela himself was groomed for the chieftainship. He started a BA degree at Fort Hare University, from which he was expelled for political activity, and he completed his degree by correspondence from Johannesburg. He helped found the ANC Youth League, and in 1952, by which time he was both Transvaal president of the ANC and deputy national president, Mandela and Oliver Tambo opened the first Black legal firm in the country. After periods of detention and military training, he was convicted and jailed for illegal travel in November 1962. While serving his sentence, he was convicted in the 'Rivonia trial' for sabotage and sentenced to life imprisonment on Robben Island (a prison that was to become a centre for learning and political education). While Mandela was not to be released until Sunday 11 February 1990, in the 1980s he was an increasingly significant interlocutor between the ANC and the regime. After his release, he played a significant role in open negotiations with the ruling National Party. He was awarded a Nobel Peace Prize in 1993 and has become recipient of an extraordinary number of honorary degrees and awards. He was inaugurated as the first democratically elected State President of South Africa on 10 May 1994.

Court. Despite brinkmanship on the part of the Inkatha Freedom Party, the negotiation process was a triumph of political management and elite control. In 1994, a few short years after negotiation began in earnest, Nelson Mandela was President of South Africa (see Box 1.4).

The chronology and conditions of creation of the final constitution provided a tidy solution to an entrenched difference between the key negotiating parties. While the NP was all along in favour of drafting the full constitution before the first election, the ANC wanted the election to create an assembly with the power to write a constitution from scratch. The inclusion of compulsory respect for Constitutional Principles – together with the safeguards offered by the principle of consensual decision-making, a government of national unity, and the constitutional court – permitted de Klerk to carry his constituency into an agreement that favoured the ANC. The ANC's additional concessions – 'sunset clauses' and pension guarantees for a vast range of state and security force employees – were a blatant and successful bribe to incumbents of state offices. (Guarantees of MPs' pensions were perhaps the most shameless and effective of such measures.) Certain legal–constitutional changes, including the end of the 'parliamentary sovereignty' inherited from

British legal thought, rendered less threatening the idea of majority rule. Confidence was cemented by the elevation of the constitution to a new status as supreme law of the land, and by the expanded role of judicial review. A number of 'fundamental rights' were inscribed in the constitution, thus placing them beyond the reach of parliamentary power. Property rights, in particular, were given firm and visible expression.

The negotiators also developed an inclusive formula for parliamentary elections which guaranteed the privileges of parliamentary membership to the elite within even the smallest parties. Inclusion was achieved by means of a broadly proportional electoral system without the cut-off for very low votes that characterizes most such systems. One seat was allocated for every quarter per cent of the vote. In the event, this proved most important in guaranteeing for the very visible Democratic Party and Pan Africanist Congress (PAC) a number of seats in Parliament for their leaders despite their tiny vote shares.

A multi-party executive was guaranteed for a transitional period; fundamental rights were defined; the potential use of emergency powers was restricted; courts with new review powers were set up; and new offices, including the Public Protector, the Human Rights Commissioners, and the Financial and Fiscal Commission were developed. Asmal notes that the 'line between fair and equitable protection of the interests of those not represented in government and the hobbling of a government with a clear popular mandate must be finely drawn' (Asmal 1995: IV) – an issue that has always been at the heart of liberal democratic political thought (see Chapter 6). However, the decisions reached were the product of extended horse-trading rather than of academic deliberation.

Conclusions

In retrospect, the early 1990s negotiations involved less brinkmanship and danger than it seemed. It should have been fairly clear who the central actors would be in South Africa's political drama. Yet, for journalists and academics in South Africa and abroad, the ANC was as unfathomable an organism as the Afrikaner establishment. The mysteries of women's, youth, civic, and church politics defied analysis. ANC-aligned unions, communists, exiles, and former political prisoners seemed comprehensible taken singly, but their sudden throwing together in a new political environment opened bewildering possibilities. The regional peculiarities of Natal (with its Indian Congress and the Inkatha Freedom Party) and of the Western Cape (with its Coloured politics and its multitude of politicized civic associations) added to the murky stew. Africanism, communism, socialism, Black Consciousness, 'charterism', and the influences of decades in exile: each left observers bewildered. Out of this confusion emerged the 1994 election, which seemed to be a miracle and the herald of a new era.

2

A Rainbow Nation

South Africa's history has bequeathed a rich ethnic, racial, linguistic, and religious diversity. In the 1996 census, of the 40.58 million population counted, 76.7 per cent classified themselves as 'African', 10.9 per cent as 'white', 8.9 per cent as 'coloured' and 2.6 per cent as 'Indian/Asian' (see Table 2.1), using designations directly descended from apartheid's notorious population registration legislation. (The South African government, while avowedly no longer supporting racial classification of the population for policy-making purposes, does use racial data to isolate trends and to identify the impacts of equity promoting policies.) However, the country's diversity transcends the racial categories of apartheid. Around one in five South Africans speak isiZulu in the home, and only slightly fewer isiXhosa. Other substantial minorities – of between 8 and 14 per cent – embrace Afrikaans, Sepedi, English, Setswana, or Sesotho as their mother tongue.

Table 2.1   Population by 'race' and mother tongue 1996

Race (self-attribution)	% of population
African	76.7
White	10.9
Coloured	8.9
Indian/Asian	2.6
Primary household language	
IsiZulu	22.9
IsiXhosa	17.9
Afrikaans	14.4
Sepedi	9.2
English	8.6
Setswana	8.2
Sesotho	7.7
Xitsonga	4.4
SiSwati	2.5
Tshivenda	2.2
IsiNdebele	1.5
Other	0.6

Source: Adapted from Statistics South Africa 2002a.

Religious affiliations include a variety of Christian denominations, Islam, Hinduism, Judaism, and traditionalist African systems of belief. Heterogeneous urban, suburban, peri-urban, township, and rural lifestyles reflect a plethora of aesthetic and cultural particularities, in addition to the country's exceptional inequalities of wealth and income. Major cities, and Johannesburg in particular, are rapidly acquiring the cosmopolitan magnificence of the great modern African metropolis.

For some scholars and political leaders, South Africa's 'deeply divided' character is her Achilles heel. For others, such as former Anglican Archbishop of Cape Town and Nobel Peace Prize-winner Desmond Tutu, the potential strength of South Africa lies in her constitution as a 'rainbow nation'. While claiming advantages for diversity, however, Tutu's characterization inadvertently highlights the degree to which the constituent colours of South Africa's rainbow have retained much of the 'apartness' they acquired during the segregationist and apartheid eras (Box 2.1).

The Entrenchment of Apartness under Apartheid

Apartheid profoundly deepened and entrenched racial and ethnic division. As we saw in Chapter 1, the entire population was classified by race and by ethnicity according to a political logic devoid of scientific coherence. A still fluid if segregated 1948 population was fully subsumed under racial categories. Only Whites were accorded full citizenship rights in the Republic of South Africa. Coloured and Asian South Africans were serviced by inferior 'own affairs' administrations, which provided for distinct and segregated public services and limited forms of political participation. Africans were attributed ethnic or tribal identities, with an officially elaborated history, language, and cultural identity. Each African ethnic group was allocated a homeland or bantustan within which the population would purportedly develop its distinct nationhood. Africans were systematically 'retribalized', stripped of South African citizenship, their civic and political rights trampled in accordance with the ambitions of the architects of the Bantustans. Hundreds of thousands of people were forcibly removed to their 'correct' locations. The segregation of space and of public amenities was pushed to new extremes.

To some degree, both racial and ethnic categories drew on pre-existing assumptions within South Africa about the nature of social division,

Box 2.1 Key facts about South Africa

Official name:	Republic of South Africa
Regime type:	Constitutional democracy
Executive capital:	Pretoria
Legislative capital:	Cape Town
Judicial capital:	Bloemfontein
Currency:	Rand
Land area:	1 219 090 square kilometres
Neighbours:	Namibia, Botswana, Zimbabwe, Mozambique, Swaziland, Lesotho
Resources:	Gold, platinum, diamonds, chromium, manganese, titanium, uranium, copper, silver, zirconium, coal
Population:	44 328 000 (2001 estimate)
of which urban:	53–57 per cent
growth rate:	2.1 per cent (1990–2000) 0.2 per cent (2000–15)
life expectancy:	52.1 (2000)
Official languages:	IsiZulu, IsiXhosa, Afrikaans, English, Sepedi, Sesotho, Setswana, SiSwati, Tshivenda, Xitsonga, IsiNdebele
Provinces:	Gauteng, KwaZulu-Natal, Western Cape, Eastern Cape, Northern Cape, Free State, Mpumalanga, Limpopo, North-West
Major '*unicities*':	Johannesburg, Cape Town, Durban, Nelson Mandela Metropole (Port Elizabeth), Tshwane (Pretoria), East Rand
HIV/AIDS prevalence:	20.1 per cent 15–49 year olds
Infant mortality:	55 per 1 000 live births

Sources: UNDP (2002), Statistics South Africa (2002a).

especially among Whites. (It is an irony of apartheid that the dark complexions of many of those who defined themselves as 'white' betrayed the pervasive cross racial sex of previous generations.) White supremacist ideology drew upon both the scientific racism of Victorian Britain, brought to South Africa by settlers in the late nineteenth century, and the frontier racism of the Boer settlers. Apartheid helped to make partially fluid conceptions of difference concrete, by forcing those with the same racial and ethnic classification to live, learn, and work together. To be a Coloured South African in the 1960s, for example, was to be labelled a member of a natural population group – one that in fact encompassed a wide variety of classes, languages, religions, and histories. Yet after three decades of forced relocation and residential segregation, Coloured South Africans, while still immensely diverse, were more alike in their self-conceptions than at apartheid's beginning. Designated Africans, for their part, have walked a fine line between pride in distinctive linguistic and cultural heritages, and abhorrence of their distortion and of the malign uses to which they were put under apartheid.

Strength from Diversity?

South Africa remains a long way from Archbishop Tutu's vision of a rainbow nation comfortable with and strengthened by its own diversity. In the remainder of this chapter, we examine five aspects of the country's heterogeneity – racial and ethnic division, language variety, religion, provincial diversity, and cosmopolitanism. We explore how they contribute or otherwise to the construction of an inclusive and coherent South African society, and how they help or hinder the creation of a common South African nationhood.

Race and Ethnicity

We have explored how the country's extended history of white supremacy, segregation and apartheid created, exacerbated, and entrenched a variety of racial and ethnic divisions. In urban areas, however, and in particular in the country's industrial heartland of Johannesburg, a cosmopolitan culture and multi-lingualism survived all attempts to impose apartheid labels. One consequence of the end of apartheid, and later the institution of non-racial democracy, has been a less politicized and more creative assertion of pride in ethnicity, nonetheless combined with a vigorous condemnation of racial divisiveness.

One central feature of ANC opposition to apartheid, moreover, was its ideology of 'non racialism', and its rejection of the implied significance of racial and ethnic labels. Given the dangers that ethnic conflict has posed in Africa, the government has approached all matters ethnic or racial cautiously since 1994. A disciplined political movement, the ANC has been historically intolerant of ethnic politicking at provincial or local level. More visibly since 1999, however, a quasi-Africanist conception of history and of politics has become increasingly prevalent in the movement's leadership, and the doctrine of non-racialism has been somewhat eroded. At times, political debate has been coarsened by the imputation of racial or ethnic motives to political opponents, particularly in the ANC centre's battles against the Inkatha Freedom Party, the Democratic Party and its own allies in the South African Communist Party and the union movement. Racialization of conflict has been an inescapable characteristic of postcolonial Southern African politics, most recently in Zimbabwe and Namibia. The roots of such politics in South Africa lie in an extended history of racial oppression. It is nevertheless fuelled by continuing racist sentiments among many historically advantaged South Africans and by the immense difficulties governments face in dismantling what appears to be a racial hierarchy of affluence and economic opportunity.

Language as a Source of Division

Critics of the emergence of English as a global language view its unfortunate rise to hegemony in South Africa as only a matter of time. However, the country will remain for many decades a site of multifaceted multi-lingualism, even if English seems likely to continue its rise as the language of government and business. The negotiators of South Africa's new political order in the early 1990s did not resolve language issues or debates over the status of ethnic groups with which languages are associated. Instead they designated eleven official languages: isiZulu, isiXhosa, isiNdebele, Sepedi, Sesotho, Setswana, siSwati, Tshivenda, Xitsonga, English, and Afrikaans. The Constitution confers the right to use the language of one's own choice and to learn in that language where this is reasonably practicable. The state's official language policy is to promote and protect linguistic and cultural diversity, and to recognize and promote multi-lingualism as a national resource.

Constitutionally guaranteed language rights are protected by the Pan South African Language Board (PANSALB) whose purpose is supposedly to promote multi-lingualism in South Africa. In practice, its role has been primarily to investigate complaints against public or private bodies that have been accused of violating any citizen's language rights. For example, an organization might discriminate against a person on the basis of his or her language, deny the right of association with members of a linguistic community, or deny a person their right to expression within their linguistic community. Complaints have come primarily from Afrikaans speakers and only a relatively small number have to date been processed. The language board has been largely incorporated into

---

Box 2.2   The land

Although South Africa is rapidly urbanizing, and her rural population has been in decline for 30 years or more, the land continues to possess a deep emotional resonance for most of her people. The country covers an area of around 1.2 million square kilometres. Two features dominate its landscape: an inland plateau that accounts for the majority of the land area, and a thin strip of coastal lowland upon which historically the population has been concentrated. Between the two rises a Great Escarpment, or set of mountain ranges, reaching in places an elevation of more than 3000 metres. The interior plateau mostly comprises grassland, shading in the Northwest into the Namib and Kalahari deserts. In the north-east it rises into the Witwatersrand ('White Waters Ridge' in Afrikaans), a gold-bearing rocky formation upon which Johannesburg was built in the great gold rush of the 1880s. In the centre of the country lie the Drakensberg mountains, at the heart of which sits the independent kingdom of Lesotho. The coastal strip, which is sometimes called the 'lowveld', is in places less than 100 kilometres in width.

---

the state and its budget is now controlled through the Department of Media, Arts, and Culture. Critics of the board question its willingness or capacity to fulfil its remit by actively promoting multi-lingualism and the protection of language rights within the society.

The 1996 census indicated that isiZulu is mother tongue of 23 per cent of the population, isiXhosa of 18 per cent, Afrikaans of 14 per cent, and Sepedi, English, Setswana, and Sesotho each of between 8 and 9 per cent (see Table 2.1). Afrikaans and English are very widespread as second languages, and English has increasingly become the language of business, the media, and politics. Nine of the official languages are 'Bantu' languages, representatives of a wider family of languages that stretches across much of sub-Saharan Africa. These languages are unsurpassed in their elegance and integrity of structure. There is very often mutual intelligibility between Bantu languages – for example, between most dialects of isiXhosa and isiZulu. Until the formalization of the languages by missionaries in the late nineteenth centuries, these tongues underwent extensive interchanges with one another and with the indigenous languages of the Khoisan and the European settlers. Young Black urban South Africans will often today speak simultaneously in Bantu, Afrikaner, and English languages, seamlessly weaving together vocabulary and grammatical structures.

Afrikaans is a formalized version of a hybrid Dutch and indigenous language patois that emerged among 'Coloureds' in the western Cape across the eighteenth and nineteenth centuries. It was both a creation of, and a vehicle for, the development of Afrikaner nationalism. In the space of just a century, in the 'miracle' of the Afrikaans language, it has developed a comprehensive vocabulary in the natural sciences and applied technologies, an extensive range of philosophical and social scientific concepts, and an impressive body of literary and poetic accomplishments.

South African English was the language of the colonial power from the start of the nineteenth century, bolstered by periodic waves of immigration from Britain, most particularly in the later nineteenth and early twentieth centuries. Dominant within national government, and the primary tongue of Whites in the Cape and Natal provinces, it was in addition the language of national government and of the major business corporations that grew out of the gold and diamond industrial revolutions. It has developed to some extent along its own trajectory, while becoming increasingly influenced by developments in American rather than British English.

Most South Africans are multi-lingual to a greater or lesser degree. African mother tongue speakers are far more likely than others to possess high level multiple language skills, often proficient in two or more secondary Bantu languages and sometimes also in the English or Afrikaans still so vital for entry into the formal labour market. Afrikaans mother tongue-speakers, by contrast, are likely to speak only English as a second tongue. English first-language speakers are those least likely to possess a second language – and where they do so it is usually Afrikaans. Language use thus continues to reflect a history (and continuing reality) in which English and Afrikaans were avenues to economic and social advancement or even for survival.

Widespread pride in the language and culture of different African language communities is accompanied by a realization that these languages were themselves used as instruments to distinguish one African 'nation' from another during the apartheid period. Few people wish to see language become once again a source or instrument of division. It is in part for this reason that English is emerging as a *de facto* national language for South Africa's middle classes, its political history excused by its status as a 'global language'.

The problems of mutual cultural accommodation and communication have been most evident at the interfaces between the historically privileged languages of English and Afrikaans and the nine new official languages. (It is no surprise that literature, poetry and the theatre, as we shall see in a later chapter, have faced extreme obstacles to advance since 1994.) Yet the continuing advantages enjoyed by English and creolized Dutch have profound consequences for the development of a coherent and inclusive social order.

There is much discussion of the blending of cultures in the new South Africa, as groups formerly set against one another by defined ethnicity and race are learning new forms of communication, consensus, and mutual adaption. Cultural defences built to protect group identities, on this view, are crumbling as South Africans learn how to treat one another's cultural practices with respect. Such new interaction is evident in the extraordinary interpenetration of languages in the everyday speech of young Black urban South Africans. Language, however, is not just the most basic instrument for the expression of cultural difference and integration. It is also the most essential precursor for desirable employment. Yet most of the country's population cannot command Afrikaans or English sufficiently well to advance in the formal labour market, and African children are profoundly disadvantaged by their need to acquire scientific and technical vocabularies through English (Alexander and Heugh 2001). While most of the urban Black population speaks several languages, many are most fluent in African tongues which do not serve as economic resources in the way English and Afrikaans continue to do.

Religion

If language continues to be a force for division, religion performs a more equivocal role. South Africa is a highly religious society. Indeed only a small minority of its population has any conception of what it might mean to live without an organized religious tradition. At the same time, there exists a great diversity of religious beliefs and practices, and an impressive tolerance of and respect for difference. Around 75 or 80 per cent of the population regard themselves as Christians, while there are substantial minorities of Hindus, Muslims, or Jews (see Table 2.2). In addition, there is a substantial body of people who consider themselves traditionalists.

The largest grouping of churches in South Africa are the African Independent Churches, descended from so-called 'Ethiopian churches' which emerged out of desertions and breakaways from mission-based religion. Primarily Zionist, Apostolic, or Pentecostal, these some 4000 independent churches have in total more than 10 million members. During the apartheid period, they played a significant if subdued political role, allowing members to articulate discontent with the racialized order and to reaffirm conceptions of social and political justice systematically disallowed in the wider society. The largest single church in South Africa,

Table 2.2   Religious affiliations (estimated 2002)

Denomination	Members (000s)	% total
Zion Christian Church	4 242	9.71
NG* Churches	3 866	8.85
Catholic	3 757	8.6
Methodist	3 080	7.05
Pentecostal/charismatic	2 416	5.53
Anglican	1 756	4.02
Apostolic Faith Mission	1 232	2.82
Lutheran	1 153	2.64
Other Zionist	2 368	5.82
Other Apostolic	3 857	8.83
Other Christian	5 251	10.62
Subtotal: Christian	32 978	75.49
Muslim	607	1.39
Hindu	590	1.35
Judaists	74	0.17
African traditional	17	0.04
Other faiths	210	0.48
Subtotal: other religions	1 503	3.44
No religion	5 089	11.65
Refused/not stated	4 111	9.41
Total population	43 686	100.00

* Dutch Reformed churches.

Source: Adapted from Institute for Missiological and Ecumenical Research, University of Pretoria; reproduced GCIS 2002: 6.

the Zion Christian Church, typifies their primarily conservative character. It has 4 million members and is notable for its annual Easter and September pilgrimages to Moria in Limpopo Province where upwards of a million church members gather for religious festivals. It has a prescriptive approach to alcohol, smoking and promiscuity, and has shunned the formulation of political programmes.

A second significant grouping of Christian churches are the Dutch Reformed churches, which altogether account for almost 4 million members celebrating primarily in the Afrikaans language. The largest reformed denomination, the Dutch Reformed Church, was closely related politically and ideologically to the Afrikaner nationalist project and in the 1950s and 1960s was sometimes labelled the 'official religion' of the National Party. Towards the end of the apartheid period, the reformed churches became conservative influences on a population that was increasingly questioning the moral coherence and political viability of the apartheid system.

African churches did not engage in open political conflict with the apartheid regime, although they gave strength and cohesion to wider community struggles. Sporadic churchmen's efforts to build an anti-apartheid political project through their religious institutions failed in the 1960 and 1970s. The (primarily Black) Methodist Church campaigned actively against apartheid, and it probably suffered significant desertions in consequence. Attempts by the leadership of the Catholic Church to formulate an anti-apartheid consensus provoked factionalism among the religion's 4 million adherents, and resulted in the emergence of a South African Catholic Defence League to protest against the integration of single-race schools. The financially robust Anglican Church opposed apartheid most consistently and unequivocally but its limited membership and identification with the English establishment militated against its effectiveness. Only through an umbrella organization – the South African Council of Churches – did many of the churches finally begin to engage in systematic protest against apartheid in the 1980s.

The Diversity of the Provinces

South Africa under apartheid consisted of four provinces – Cape Province, Natal, Transvaal, and Orange Free State – together with 10 designated 'homelands' allocated to African 'nations' in accordance with the high apartheid ideology of separate development. In the political settlement reached in 1993, as the country approached its first non-racial franchise election the following year, nine provinces were delineated. This new organization of the provinces involved the incorporation of Bantustans, and the breaking down of some geographically large provinces, notably the Cape, into more appropriate vehicles for service delivery and political accountability. Each of the nine provinces contains a diversity of population, economic activity, and culture.

Wide variations in economic performance, job availability, and population structure divide the provinces. Jobs are extremely scarce in the rural provinces and poverty is widespread. Former 'homelands', moreover, act as nurseries for the young and the homes of the old – in Gauteng the dependency ratio (of non-working to working age) is below 50:100 while in Limpopo it is above 100:100. Other than Gauteng, which is by far the most densely populated area in South Africa, population has been most concentrated in the poorest areas of South Africa's interior, especially in Bantustans to which Africans were confined by apartheid legislation. Over the past decade, however, the urbanization characteristic of developing countries has accelerated as apartheid era 'displaced urbanization' to high-density Bantustan settlements is reversed. At least half the population lives in urban areas (perhaps more than 60 per cent on less legalistic definitions of 'urban' that include high-density informal settlements and ex-homeland conurbations). Even on a narrow definition, urbanization is expected to rise to 56 per cent by 2015 and 65 per cent by 2030 (DFID 2001: 45). These figures again disguise considerable regional variation. Gauteng is currently 97 per cent urban, and the Western Cape 89 per cent, whereas Free State and Northern Cape have 70 per cent urbanization levels. Eastern Cape, KwaZulu Natal, Mpumalanga, Limpopo, and the North-West are between 35 and 45 per cent urbanized (Statistics South Africa 2002a: 8).

The economic heartland of South Africa, Gauteng is the country's most dynamic province and contains its highest population density. It accounts for around 40 per cent of South Africa's GDP and contains both Johannesburg – Southern Africa's most populous city – and the country's executive capital Pretoria. Its population of around 8 million is almost entirely urbanized and contains an unusually high proportion of young and educated South Africans. Johannesburg is the centre of inward migration into South Africa, primarily from elsewhere on the African continent, and the city is highly cosmopolitan. Many of the business headquarters and offices that grew up in Johannesburg have migrated northwards to the area of Sandton, which was the venue for the 2002 World Summit on Sustainable Development. The city centre has become home to businesses and migrants from around Africa.

Like other parts of South Africa, the province continues to exhibit the residential segregation by race that characterized apartheid. In this tiny province, comprising only 1.4 per cent of the country's land area, the republic's most wealthy citizens live in close proximity to some of its poorest. South of the city lies Soweto (South Western Townships), home to around 2 million people, yet not quite a city in itself because of its dependency upon the economy, services, and employment possibilities of Johannesburg. All of the townships in the Gauteng are characterized by a very high degree of linguistic and cultural diversity, and the population is of exceptional political sophistication.

South Africa's most populous province, KwaZulu-Natal (or KZN) contains around 9 million people and accounts for about 15 per cent of GDP. It hosts the country's major port of Durban, and it has a diversified and dynamic economy. Eighty per cent of its population are isiZulu

---

Box 2.3   HIV/AIDS and population growth

In 1976 South Africa contained just 26 million people. The population today, after three decades of rapid growth, is more than 44 million. More than half of all South Africans are under the age of 25. If these bald statistics are indicative of the dynamic population growth typical in any developing country, projections for the next decade tell a more gloomy tale. HIV/AIDS is expected to bring this expansion to a complete halt and growth is unlikely to resume until 2015 (UNDP 2002: 164). While life expectancy at birth was 56.7 between 1995 and 2000, up from 53.7 between 1970 and 1975, actuarial projections indicate that it will fall steadily across the next decade, bottoming out at around 40 by 2011 (ASSA 2002). Because HIV is primarily spread through sexual contact, its incidence is especially high among young adults. For this reason, South Africa's 'dependency ratio' between those of working age and others will worsen sharply. A smaller working population – much of which is suffering HIV/AIDS-related illness – will have to support a heavier burden of young and old dependants.

---

speakers, with the remainder primarily mother-tongue speakers of English. Around 8 million South Africans consider themselves Zulu, and KZN is home to the majority of Zulu-speakers. It is also the political heartland of the Inkatha Freedom Party (IFP), South Africa's only major ethnic-based political movement. The IFP has a history of conflict with the ANC in the province, with the ANC historically tending to represent more urbanized and less traditionalist Zulu-speakers – whether within the province or in Gauteng where a very substantial Zulu-speaking population lives. The leader of the IFP, Mangosuthu Buthelezi, participated from the outset in the post-1994 Government of National Unity (GNU), and he remains a member of Thabo Mbeki's cabinet holding the portfolio of Minister of Home Affairs. The co-operative relationship between IFP and ANC has contributed to markedly reduced levels of political violence in the province, but the two parties remain locked in a struggle for votes and patronage.

KZN also contains a considerable Indian-descended population of around 1 million. Many of these South Africans trace their ancestry to indentured sugar plantation labourers, brought to Natal from the south of India in the late nineteenth century, but others were later voluntary migrants from central and northern India. Most of these Indians are English language speakers, although other languages flourish in many households. Around 60 per cent are Hindus with the remainder mostly Muslim or Christian. The experience of classification and segregation in the apartheid period has helped to reduce the significance of class and cultural differentiation among Indians, but it has not led to any major independent political organization. KZN also contains the descendants of a substantial wave of British migrants in the mid-nineteenth century who quickly moved to the larger towns and established a dominance over business and trade. KZN is notable today for its exceptionally high HIV prevalence – estimated by some to be as high as 20 per cent for the provincial population as a whole, or around 30 per cent for adults aged between 20 and 65. AIDS deaths already outstrip non-AIDS deaths and life expectancy may fall to the mid-30s over the next decade.

The Western Cape is the third major economic centre of South Africa, accounting for some 15 per cent of GDP despite its population of only around 4.2 million. Around 60 per cent of this population are Afrikaans-speaking with the remainder equally divided between isiXhosa and English speakers. It has a well-diversified economy, with great potential in tourism, and enjoys the lowest unemployment rates in the country at about 15 per cent. The majority of the Western Cape's population were designated 'coloureds' under apartheid. This category referred to an heterogeneous collection of people brought together by their failure to fit into the 'African' versus 'European' typologies around which apartheid was elaborated. Many Coloured South Africans speak English as a first language or are fully bilingual, although a majority would describe Afrikaans as their mother-tongue. There is a diversity of religious beliefs within the Coloured community.

Some Coloured Western Cape inhabitants trace their ancestry to the Griqua, a society of largely Khoisan and Afrikaner descent with a three century long history of political organization and displacement. Like most Coloured people, this group are Dutch Reformed Church adherents and speak primarily Afrikaans. Others, sometimes labelled 'Cape Malays', are Muslims descended variously from Malaysian, Afrikaner, and Khoikhoi peoples, and the various slave populations that passed through the Cape. As with Indian South Africans in KZN, the common experience of apartheid oppression – combined with the greater economic and political freedom of Coloured than African – created a complex heritage of community self-recognition and pride together with ambivalence about politics. Coloured people in the Western Cape have been among the most militant and determined opponents of apartheid but also delivered to the National Party, apartheid's creator, a provincial election victory over the ANC in the 1994 foundational election.

South Africa's remaining six provinces have distinctive characters but each is blighted by high levels of poverty and immense developmental challenges. Eastern Cape is South Africa's poorest but perhaps most beautiful province, its 7 million inhabitants – alongside Gauteng's – the country's most politically sophisticated. Its primarily isiXhosa speaking population has the longest history of interaction with settler and colonial powers, and European missionaries and teachers became an established presence over the nineteenth century. As early as the turn of the twentieth century, most of South Africa's emerging Black professionals, primarily ministers, doctors, and lawyers ('iiqwetha' meaning twisters or deceivers in Xhosa), came from the area today occupied by Eastern Cape. (IsiXhosa speakers, notably Nelson Mandela and Thabo Mbeki, have also been prominent in national politics.) Its economy is heavily dependent on the motor manufacturing sector but it has the potential to develop a substantial tourism industry.

Northern Cape is a vast and sparsely populated semi-arid province whose economy is centred on sheep farming, mining, and fisheries. The Free State, lying at the centre of South Africa, has a population of less than 3 million primarily Sotho speaking people distributed over almost 130 000 square kilometres. The province's relatively limited income is primarily derived from mining, manufacturing, and agriculture (particularly field crops). The mining industry is the province's biggest employer and the goldfield region of Free State accounts for almost a third of South Africa's gold output. In addition there are productive diamond mines. These industries have fallen upon very hard times, however, and the Free

---

Box 2.4   Climate

South Africa has a mostly temperate climate. The interior plateau is characterized by long hours of sunshine and warm days, and cool but rarely cold nights. Summer temperatures are normally in the high 20 or early 30 degrees centigrade. Rainfall occurs primarily in the summer, between November and March. While it varies considerably from region to region, and within the coastal belt, average annual rainfall in the North and East is sufficient at between 478 millimetres (Limpopo) and 844 millimetres (KwaZulu Natal) to support crop production. Rainfall in the West can support only livestock farming. There are some exceptional climatic zones. The area immediately around Cape Town has a Mediterranean climate, with heavy winter rather than summer rainfall; the North West is very dry and includes an area of desert; and the far North and north-east have subtropical conditions with substantially higher summer temperatures than the highveld and Rand.

State is suffering a crisis of falling incomes and plummeting formal sector employment.

In the North of South Africa lie three geographically smaller provinces: North-West Province, Mpumalanga, and Limpopo (formerly Northern Province). Two-thirds of North West's primarily Setswana-speaking population of 3.6 million live in rural areas, and the provincial economy is based on minerals and agriculture. Mpumalanga's 3 million population is concentrated on an area of less than 80 000 square kilometres, and contains substantial mother-tongue populations of siSwati, isiZulu, and isiNdebele. The region is famous for its tourist routes and citrus fruits, but its economy is dominated by its coal reserves and it contains the country's biggest power stations (with resultant high levels of air pollution).

Limpopo Province, perhaps surpassing even Eastern Cape in its natural beauty, rivals it also in its poverty. More than half of its 5.5 million people are Sepedi speakers, but the province embraces a variety of languages including Xitsonga and Tshivenda. Limpopo incorporates several troubled apartheid era Bantustans within its borders, and it has experienced difficulties converting its immense economic potential into enhanced welfare for its population. It is likely, however, to be one of South Africa's major sites of economic growth across the next decade.

The system of provincial government, as we shall see in Chapter 6, has both political and service delivery roles. While many have been critical of the slow transformation of public services at provincial level – particularly the health and education services managed by provincial administrations – they have performed relatively well as the vehicles for political competition in a polity dominated at national level by the ANC.

Migration and Xenophobia

In addition to the variety of populations bequeathed by its history, South Africa also contains a diverse immigrant and refugee population of more recent origin from elsewhere in Africa. Estimates of this mostly illegal immigrant population fall between 2 and 8 million. Regional instability, in particular in Zimbabwe, presents the possibility of further substantial cross-border migration in future years. On the whole, South Africans have not responded well to the recent increase in immigration. Despite widespread Africanist rhetoric, xenophobia is rampant, and most venomous when directed towards fellow Africans. In Gauteng, where substantial entrepreneurial immigrant communities have purportedly threatened the livelihoods of local street traders and small businesspeople, there have been many reports of violence and intimidation. Anecdotal evidence suggests that the Home Affairs department deals in an arbitrary manner with refugee and work permit applications from the nationals of other African states. It may be that such tensions will abate over time, as the economic benefits of a new sub-continental commercial community become apparent. Johannesburg, already southern Africa's largest city, is tied by its human networks into the major commercial centres of the continent.

South African emigration has also been substantial in recent years (Crush and McDonald 2003). More than 200 000 South Africans left permanently for English-speaking countries alone between 1989 and 1997, and analysts predict the next five years might see anywhere between 30 000 and 200 000 further departures. Émigrés, usually beneficiaries of South Africa's highly unequal educational provision, often bewail the limitations of the new South Africa in order to ease the guilt of exile.

Contrary to conventional wisdom, it is not South Africa's Whites alone who are leaving the country or considering doing so. It is professionals of all races and ethnicities, often citing crime or limited job opportunities, who are contemplating such moves. The government has recently begun to recognize that emigrants can be a resource rather than merely a 'brain drain'. Returning migrants bring back with them skills and contacts'. Those leaving permanently often retain a profound interest in South Africa, and have the potential to develop business relationships over the long term. It is always difficult, however, to transmute the bitterness of departure into a positive disposition towards a country of birth.

The government has not so far developed a satisfactory policy for managing population movements into and out of South Africa. In common with many other states, South Africa does not have an immigration or emigration strategy designed to minimize the economic harm caused by skills loss or to maximize the benefits that immigration and a benevolent Diaspora can bring. Xenophobia has limited legal in-migration to a few thousand per year with the potential economic benefits of the immigration of skilled workers from elsewhere in Africa disregarded. After almost a decade of policy confusion, there remains little likelihood of a coherent migration strategy developing.

Conclusions

Uprooting an entrenched sense of apartness remains one of South Africa's greatest challenges. The constitution enjoins the citizenry of the

---

Box 2.5 The Truth and Reconciliation Commission

Meeting first in April 1996, and submitting its final report to President Thabo Mbeki only in March 2003, the Truth and Reconciliation Commission (TRC) had a threefold mandate. It was charged to investigate and report upon apartheid-era human rights violations; to grant amnesty to admitted perpetrators who had fully disclosed their actions; and to make recommendations concerning reparations. The TRC's principal achievement was to elicit and record the testimony of thousands of victims of human rights violations, and to establish on the historical record the extent and nature of such abuses committed during the era of political struggle. However, the ANC, IFP, and NP each selectively challenged the TRC's findings and so undermined its credibility. The institutional executors of apartheid – in business, the media, the judiciary, and the universities – avoided admission of (and so reflection upon) their own culpability. Individual perpetrators of abuse only rarely disclosed their actions and sought amnesty, and victims' testimony is likely only very exceptionally to support prosecutions. The government moved very slowly towards a reparations policy, announcing in 2003 that the victims of humans rights abuses are to receive only modest consolatory payments.

---

new democracy to recognize the injustices of the past and to heal the divisions of history. Yet even after a seven year 'truth and reconciliation' process citizens remain divided over, as well as by, their history. Some still view South Africa as 'two nations' – White and Black – divided by culture, wealth, and history. As we shall see in Chapter 4, however, a more complex reality contains a substantial non-White middle-class, growing levels of intra-Africa inequality, and a diversity of White living standards. Nonetheless, almost all of the poor in South Africa are African, and almost all of the rich are White. Changes in the labour market and employment patterns, moreover, have resulted in a growing gulf between the wealthiest in the society, who are predominantly White, and the poorest and the unemployed, who are overwhelmingly Black. Given the country's history of racialized political division, such a situation is not tenable in the longer term.

Middle-class South Africans are building a degree of social harmony across racial divides. Everyday personal interaction is marked by the courtesy that often accompanies social division. At the same time, a society that never permitted interaction across racial boundaries on remotely equal terms is starting to do so. It is developing in its educational institutions, its public sector, and its private businesses the new forms of common understanding that can only come from personal experience and communication.

However, an asymmetry of power and wealth still almost always accompanies South Africans' relationships across races. They often seem to be guided by racial stereotypes and the potential for politicization of racial difference is everywhere evident. In the past, the ANC's doctrine of non-racialism has been a bulwark against the political abuse of racial difference. Yet the failure of government and the privileged to change the structures of racial disadvantage may one day create fertile ground for a new generation of political entrepreneurs willing to exploit racial discord. The xenophobia that greets many of Gauteng's African economic migrants is no substitute for the sense of nationhood and social inclusion that South Africans are striving unevenly to attain.

3
The South African Economy

Introduction

The South African economy seems beset by paradoxes. It is the largest in the region, with higher output than the rest of Southern Africa combined. Yet, in global terms, it is a dwarf. It is the most advanced economy on the African continent. Nevertheless, it suffers from massive shortfalls in skills and infrastructure. Home to sophisticated financial services and information technology companies, it still contains a significant minerals sector that emerged in the late nineteenth century. Its affluent suburbs and blatant consumerism rub shoulders with an impoverished peri-urban poor. This uneven urban prosperity is divided by a chasm of inequality from South Africa's rural dispossessed who endure a poverty that would not be out of place in one of the world's very poorest nations.

Yet many of these often remarked paradoxes are less puzzling than they first seem. Middle-income developing countries routinely display extreme contrasts in economic development, with high technology business and wealthy urban elites coexisting with extreme poverty and economic backwardness. South Africa is by no means the only state in the South to remain wedded to its economic past as a primary sector resource extractive economy. Its seeming achievements, moreover, are exaggerated by the desperate history of disappointment that has plagued the continent. As we shall see in Chapter 4, it is only in the country's terrible and multi-faceted inequality that its record is truly outstanding.

Output and Expenditure

The total value of goods and services produced in 2001 was a little over R975 billion ($/Euro 100 billion), the highest output of any country on the African continent (Statistics South Africa 2002a: 31). With a little over 7 per cent of Africa's population, the country is responsible for more than one-third of its output of goods and services. To place this achievement in context, however, the country's output amounts to less than 2 per cent that of the United States economy.

GDP growth followed an unexceptional developing country trajectory for the first three of the past five decades (Moll 1990). An extended boom began before the Second World War, at the end of which manufacturing overtook the primary sector as the largest part of the economy. Rapid advance continued through the 1950s, with average growth of 4 per cent per annum, and into the 1960s with yearly growth at almost 6 per cent. In common with most other developing countries, South Africa's economic trajectory headed downwards sharply in the mid-1970s as the first of the major post-war international recessions was triggered by the increase in international oil prices. Thereafter, however, in the 1980s and early 1990s, GDP growth was heavily influenced by country-specific factors, such as changes in commodity (and especially gold) prices, and the political crises and international disinvestment that resulted from the struggle for a non-racial democracy. In the 1980s, growth averaged less than 1.5 per cent, and the 1990s scarcely improved upon this disappointing rate.

Since 1994, the country has enjoyed positive but quite low levels of economic growth (see Table 3.1). While any growth in a difficult global economic climate has been an achievement, it has been accompanied by steady population expansion. This has virtually eliminated per capita GDP growth. In addition, South Africa's growth has been 'jobless growth', with the number of people employed in formal non-agricultural employment falling between 1994 and 2000. There are indications, however, that a more favourable set of conditions is now in place. The productive potential of the economy may well grow faster than the 3 per cent ceiling that has recently confined it, although few think the

Table 3.1   Economic growth 1996–2001

	GDP 1995 Rand*	% growth
1996	571 706	4.3
1997	586 838	2.6
1998	591 309	0.8
1999	603 842	2.1
2000	628 129	3.4
2001	638 010	2.2

* GDP at constant 1995 prices (Rand millions).
Source: Adapted from National Treasury 2002.

5 or 6 per cent growth that would make substantial inroads into the country's unemployment crisis is likely to be realized. Like any emerging economy, South Africa remains highly vulnerable to external conditions that it cannot control or even very much influence.

South Africa's late nineteenth century mining and agriculture dominated economy became progressively a manufacturing economy, with manufacturing exceeding other sectors by the mid-twentieth century. Services have achieved greater significance across the past three decades. The country entered the twenty-first century a reasonably diversified and robust economy, dominated by the services sector (65 per cent) with the secondary sector (including manufacturing) accounting for 20 per cent and the primary sector for only 13 per cent. Manufacturing, finance, and government are the three biggest industrial categories (see Figure 3.1).

Despite this shift towards a more diversified economy, some scholars argue that resources remain at the heart of the economy. While mining itself accounts for only 5.8 per cent of GDP (Statistics South Africa 2002a: 33), there are strong relationships between mining and sectors such as electricity, non-metallic minerals products, iron and steel industries, fertilizers, pesticides, chemicals, and petroleum industries. For this reason, some analysts claim a 'minerals–energy complex' still accounts for a fifth or even a quarter of the output of the economy (Fine and Rustomjee 1996).

Figure 3.1   Contribution of various industries to GDP, 2001

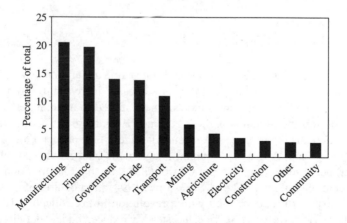

Source: Adapted from Statistics South Africa 2002a.

Economic Policy Framework

The ANC has adopted an orthodox and conservative policy framework since 1994. The government's overall macro-economic framework – elaborated in 1996 as the Growth, Employment and Redistribution strategy (GEAR) – emphasizes the pursuit of economic stability, market-friendly policy, and fiscal discipline as the prerequisites for sustained economic growth. A stable environment for private investment, the attraction of foreign investors, labour market flexibility, industrial policy, and partially privatized public assets are policies that according to GEAR will create the potential for a faster growing economy with higher levels of employment. GEAR has been controversial within the ANC and especially among its tripartite alliance partners, the Congress of South African Trade Unions (COSATU) and the South African Communist Party (SACP). COSATU has complained that GEAR entrenches unemployment and has so far delivered few pay-offs in return for its conservative macro-economic position. While the government has recently reaffirmed in the strongest possible terms its commitment to GEAR, it has moved towards a more interventionist micro-economic strategy, an expanded industrial policy, and the creation of more elaborate systems of social welfare support to ameliorate the implications of economic restructuring for the poor. These interventionist strategies build on the tradition of a Reconstruction and Development Programme (RDP) which from 1994 embodied the developmental aspirations of the left of the ANC. Employment creation, an especially significant part of this new orientation of policy, is discussed in the next chapter.

Monetary and Fiscal Policy

From the mid-1970s, as the apartheid state came under increasing political and economic stress, fiscal policy became increasingly erratic as public expenditure and finance departments failed to maintain effective control over outlays and tax revenue. Since 1994, there has been a transformation on both revenue and expenditure sides of the budget. From 1987 to 1991, South Africa was running budget deficits of around 10 billion Rand per annum, around 5 per cent of GDP, and this rose to around 10 per cent of GDP in 1992 and 1993. Since 1994, strict control of government expenditure, combined with a revolution in tax collection by the South African Revenue Service, has steadily reduced budget deficits first to 4 per cent in 1997, then to 3.2 per cent in 2000 and 2 per cent in 2001.

In addition, a reforming and activist Finance Ministry has moved to make the budgetary process more transparent, and initiated a bold shift from incremental to zero-based budgeting. It is following the international trend towards an accrual-based system, in which the true effects of expenditure and revenue changes are reflected in the year they are made. Through the introduction of a rolling three-year medium-term expenditure framework in 1998, the government has also moved to reduce uncertainty and increase the ability of economic actors to plan reliably for the future.

Monetary policy aims to secure a stable financial environment within which economic decisions are no longer influenced by variable and high inflation. Under the 1996 constitution, monetary policy is the joint responsibility of the Ministry of Finance and the South African Reserve Bank. In 2000, this joint authority agreed to adopt mechanisms of formal inflation rate targeting, with an initial target band of 3–6 per cent. The Reserve Bank's Monetary Policy Committee, consisting of Reserve Bank governors and officials, is charged with adjusting monetary policy to bring inflation into line with its target range. The Reserve Bank also oversees the banking system as a whole, and acts as the central bank of South Africa.

One especially contentious responsibility of the Reserve Bank is its administration of the country's system of exchange controls. These instruments limit the amounts of capital South African businesses and citizens are permitted to move offshore. The government is committed to a gradual relaxation of these controls and ultimately to an open capital market, goals to which it has moved by means of increasingly generous allowances and technical mechanisms through which business and individuals are able to move capital. The government's gradualist approach has recently received the full support of the International Monetary Fund.

Industrial Policy and Integrated Development Policies

The government continues to proclaim the primary importance of fiscal and monetary stability, and to stress the priority it gives to market-friendly and competition-enhancing policies. Its competition policy, as expressed in the *Competition Act* (RSA 1998) aims to reduce opportunities for restrictive practices, the abuse of market dominance, and corruption. However, the South African government has also moved to establish a relatively ambitious industrial strategy. The Department of Trade and

Industry has a *Support Programme for Industrial Promotion* to promote technology development in manufacturing industry, and spatial development initiatives, designed to unlock economic potential in areas of socio-economic deprivation and to develop economic relations with neighbouring states. The most innovative (if unproven) elements of industrial policy concern micro-business promotion, through which the country's estimated three million micro-enterprises – businesses employing five or fewer workers – are to be provided progressively with technical support and advice.

Notwithstanding these initiatives, South Africa is a developing country without a clear framework for development. Responsibility for developmental issues is distributed within and between government departments and between institutions at different levels of government. Departments such as Trade and Industry, Social Development, Agriculture, Land Affairs, Health, Transport, Housing, Water Affairs and Forestry, and Public Works, and key parastatals such as Eskom and Telkom, have not yet found a way of working together. The different 'spheres' of government – national, provincial, and especially local government – will also have to work more effectively together if developmental strategies are to succeed. For these reasons, a major focus of government, under the responsibility of the Department of Provincial and Local Government and the Presidency, has been on elaborating integrated developmental

---

Box 3.1   Key facts about South Africa's economy (2000)

GDP (US$ billions)	125.9
GDP (PPP* US$ billions)	402.4
GDP per capita (PPP US$)	9401
% living on < $1 per day (1993)	11.5%
Imports as % GDP	26%
Exports as % GDP	29%
Primary exports as % merchandised exports	33%
High technology % manufactured exports	1%
Public spending on education as % GDP**	7.6%
Military expenditure as % GNP	1.5%
Debt service as % GNP	3.1%

* Purchasing power parity figures (PPP) adjust for price differentials between countries for purposes of comparison.
** 1995–97 figures.

Sources: UNDP 2002; Statistics South Africa 2002a.

strategies for both urban and rural areas, and on building the capacity of municipalities. An *Integrated Sustainable Rural Development Programme* and an urban renewal strategy, however, focus on a relatively small number of 'nodal points' in which it is hoped concerted action by government can make a substantial difference to developmental outcomes. Further resources are likely to be released for such activities across the next decade.

Trade and Internationalization

South Africa's exports across the twentieth century were dominated to an unusual extent by a single commodity: gold. This over-dependence, which a variety of government policies failed to correct, left the currency subject to commodity-related swings in value, a property that itself served to further weaken export-oriented manufacturing. Despite a range of incentives and infrastructural provisions for export-oriented industry, gold (and then gold and platinum) continued to account for almost 40 per cent of external revenues. Imports have been dominated in the post-war period by industrial inputs (such as machinery), automobiles, chemicals, and oil.

Primary product demand has declined over recent decades, South Africa has re-entered a liberalizing global economy, and its currency has depreciated steadily. Together, these factors have brought about a substantial shift in the composition and volume of exports. Since 1994, both exports and imports in manufactured goods have demonstrated very strong upward trends, and the export base has diversified impressively.

European countries remain the major trading partners and investment sources and recipients for South Africa. Germany, and the United Kingdom are South Africa's second and third largest trading partners, and are major sources of investment, while relations are also strong with France, Switzerland, Belgium, Sweden, Denmark, and Italy. The United States is another key trading partner for South Africa, and represents an especially important area for export growth in the aftermath of the *African Growth and Opportunity Act*, which allows duty-free export of specified products. South Africa has negotiated special trading relationships with the European Union and the United States, and it is also deepening trade and investment relations with Eastern European countries, Japan (which is South Africa's fourth-largest trading partner), Malaysia, and Latin America.

The focus of the Mbeki Presidency, however, has been on the development of economic relationships within the African continent. Around a third of South Africa's exports are destined for other African states, while the Republic is also a major source of foreign direct investment for many other African countries, especially members of the Southern African Development Community (SADC). Energy and transport parastatals, mining groups, agro-processers, retailers, and brewers have been among those businesses pursuing aggressive investment and acquisition strategies in Africa since 1994.

Through the New Partnership for Africa's Development (NEPAD), it is hoped that South African businesses will benefit from increasing external interest in the economies of the continent. However, NEPAD's currently diffuse mandate – addressing trade issues, debt relief, aid co-ordination, infrastructure investment, foreign direct investment, and conflict resolution – will require clarification if it is to endear itself to major western partners in the G8, the EU, and the World Bank. When NEPAD becomes integrated in the structures of the African Union, probably in 2004 or 2005, it is likely to have a narrower focus on international trade negotiations and market access, the rationalization of Africa's own regional economic and trading communities, and development aid (see Chapter 8).

Investment Flows

While South Africa was the recipient of very considerable inward flows of capital to both mining and manufacturing sectors in the 1960s it became increasingly dependent on loan capital which itself dried up as the country's political situation worsened in the 1980s. Since 1994, there has been a resurgence of portfolio or indirect investment, with R200 billion flowing into the Johannesburg Stock Exchange between 1994 and 1998 alone. However, direct investment has involved far smaller sums, and perhaps two-thirds of this has been in mergers and acquisitions rather than into the greenfield investment that most directly expands capacity and creates employment and output (Muradzikwa 2002).

This is a problem for the African continent as a whole. While global foreign direct investment in 2000 amounted to some US$865 billion, only a little over 1 per cent of this amount came to the African continent, with South Africa receiving just US$1.4 billion. Such disappointments have preoccupied South African policy makers. Some opinion formers complain bitterly about this shortfall in foreign direct investment which it had been widely hoped might compensate for low levels of domestic saving and provide access to technology, knowledge, managerial capacity, financial markets, and international distribution networks. Some critics complain that poorly informed international investors have been unduly swayed by negative press sentiment and exaggerated perceptions of African crisis, and have proven unable to differentiate South Africa from its northern neighbours.

South African opinion formers can be classified in three ways with regard to this issue: ultra-critics, moderates, and liberal sceptics. The smallest group, the ultra-critics, accuse international business and finance of unfounded Afro-pessimism and implicit racism. Blaming OECD-zone business people's intractable prejudices for weak inward investment, ultra-critics in the ANC and its allies sometimes (and largely for domestic consumption) advocate protectionism, non-co-operation with international organizations, and special economic relationships with like-thinking partners elsewhere in the developing world.

Moderates complain that the country is unjustly associated with (purported) 'African' economic and social ailments – corruption, authoritarian leadership, and tribalism – and point to evidence that investors take an undifferentiated view of the performance of Africa's economies (Bhinda *et al.* 1999; UNCTAD 1999). These moderates argue that South Africa should work – when appropriate with African partners – to confront negative perceptions, cement relationships with international businesses, and reshape foreigners' and expatriates' perceptions of South Africa. They argue for a 'business-friendly' policy framework comparable to that in developing countries elsewhere, and sometimes for additional orthodox initiatives, such as spatial development plans, business promotion agencies, investment drives, and tax incentives. The more cautious focus on enhancing the developmental impact of investment that does materialize, and on courting new investors where specific investment opportunities and partners have been identified.

Liberal sceptics – a tiny minority within the ANC but representing business orthodoxy – tend to disparage activist prescriptions with regard to perceptions or sentiment. They argue that South Africa is in fact fortunate to enjoy today's levels of investor interest. Such sceptics stress that South Africa is a medium sized economy in a small region, locked into a slow growth path, and that these features represent the decisive impediments to investment. Foreign direct investors, like the domestic actors from whom they often take their cues, are not very susceptible to misinformation or misperception. They take business decisions on narrow business grounds, and will continue to adopt defensive strategies – such as telescoped business plans, local borrowing, and the immediate repa-triation of profits – so long as South African conditions demand them. Such sceptics argue that the government should focus its attention, not on 'perceptions' or 'uncertainty', but on objective and remediable obsta-cles to doing business: inherited structural weaknesses, uneven infra-structure, unskilled, expensive and unionized labour, crime, corruption, and a host of others. The moderate position is likely to continue to dom-inate in the ANC. Senior policy makers are reconciled to prevailing international orthodoxy about prudent government. At the same time, like their counterparts elsewhere on the continent, South African intellectuals have been unremitting critics of the injustice and political domination that is integral to the international economic order.

Public and Private Sectors

South Africa's qualified but determined accommodation of international intellectual orthodoxy is also found in the government's approach to the role of the state in a modern economy. From 1948, parastatals were used as the engines of the Afrikaner nationalist project, driving up the living standards of Afrikaners both through public service provision and through employment creation. Key state-owned enterprises today include Eskom, Transnet, and Telkom, each of which has a turnover of around R20 billion. Together they employ around 200 000 people.

The next three largest state-owned enterprises are the Industrial Development Corporation, The Development Bank of Southern Africa, and the Land Bank of South Africa, which have combined assets of around R35 billion and immense leverage over both urban and rural development. In addition there are a number of smaller parastatals, including Denel (for-merly Armscor), Rand Water, the Post Office, the Airports Company, and the South African Broadcasting Corporation. There has been extensive restructuring in the parastatal sector, with managed liberalization and rationalization in transport, energy, and telecommunications. Despite heavy resistance from the trade union movement, the government is likely to push ahead with partial privatization in almost all sectors over the next five years.

In contrast to this general retreat of the state, public works pro-grammes are likely to undergo expansion in the face of alarming levels of unemployment and associated poverty. The institutional and financial obstacles to a social security welfare net seem insuperable. The Community-Based Public Works Programme targets areas of exceptional poverty in rural areas, and maximizes employment creation and capacity building, particularly among women. Among other effective employment creation and poverty alleviation measures is the Working for Water programme, led by the Department of Water Affairs and Forestry, a labour intensive scheme for the clearance of 'alien vegetation' which can potentially affect water security, ecological systems, and the prevalence of fire and flood. The programme employs almost 20 000 people annually.

Most notable among the government's initiatives has been an increase in partnerships between private, public, and voluntary sectors. Recent initiatives have recognized the importance of voluntary work in supporting the poorest of the country's communities and in enhancing the personal security and well-being of the aged and ill. The HIV/AIDS pandemic will make such voluntarism still more important across the next decade in the absence of an appropriate health and welfare infrastructure. In a number of areas – water and sanitation, waste removal, electricity generation and reticulation, prison construction and management, education, and toll road construction – the government has also embraced the concept of public–private partnerships. There is much scope for further partnerships in rail and harbour redevelopment, government property upgrading and development, and energy generation. In addition, the government has worked increasingly systematically with local and international non-governmental organizations in the provision of public services.

Private finance initiatives, however, have been the object of unremitting scorn from the trade union movement, and this has exacerbated tensions within the ANC–SACP–COSATU alliance. Such projects often bring considerable problems, most notably in the exclusion of the very poor from effective participation as market actors. However, while market imperfections and failures will be an inevitable consequence of public–private partnerships, especially in a context of extreme inequality, the public sector suffers equally from an inability to finance and execute such projects and partnerships will often remain the least worst option.

Selected Sectors of the Economy

Resources, Extractive Industries and Energy

The modern South African state was created by the late nineteenth-century minerals revolutions. While extraction remains technically difficult, South Africa has around half of all known gold reserves and continues to account for 30 or 40 per cent of world gold output. The fortunes of the South African economy have been closely related to the price of gold, and this has brought an unhappy degree of instability to the country's economic environment. Gold has also been blamed by some historians for the political trajectory of apartheid. Always dependent on extremely low cost labour, some analysts claim that the migrant labour system – in which workers would be employed on short contracts in the prime of their working lives, while their families, children, and old people languished in the reserves – was a direct product of the gold economy.

Over the twentieth century, the country experienced a diversification of mining activity. By the middle of the century, South Africa was one of the world's largest producers of a whole range of materials: gold, platinum, diamonds, chromium, manganese, titanium, vermiculite, zirconium, vanadium, uranium, copper, silver, and asbestos. In addition, South Africa has immense reserves of coal – which have supported its energy generation industries and a host of related energy-intensive industries – as well as considerable reserves of iron ore. Platinum group metals now equal or even surpass the contribution of gold to the economy. In 2000, total sales of gold amounted to some R25 billion (Euro/$2.5), while sales of platinum group metals totalled R27 billion. Coal sales totalled some R20 billion, and base and ferrous minerals around R5 billion each. Other minerals amounted to some R15 billion in sales. Official figures indicate that the mining industry contributed 5–7 per cent to GDP in 2000, but perhaps 15 per cent through associated multiplier effects. Mining also employs some 400 000 people on 750 mines. The industry indirectly supports many tens of thousands of other employees. A little under R25 billion in wages was paid out in this sector in 2000. Stakeholders, including the Chamber of Mines, the National Union of Mineworkers, and the government's Department of Minerals Affairs and Energy, have striven together to maintain the viability of marginal mines and to safeguard employment in this sector.

South Africa suffers strategic energy dilemmas. It has very significant coal reserves, perhaps 55 or 60 million tons, equal to 10 per cent of the global total, or the fifth largest known amount. In addition, it has substantial uranium resources. However, it has almost no petroleum and is therefore vulnerable to oil price fluctuation. Electricity generation, almost entirely by parastatal Eskom, is primarily based on coal reserves in the north of the country. Due to substantial over investment in the 1970s and 1980s, and slow economic growth in the past two decades, there is currently oversupply of generating capacity. Energy prices for industry are consequently very low, encouraging the development of energy-intensive industries (see Chapter 4).

Manufacturing and Finance

South Africa's reasonably diverse manufacturing base has weathered the difficult decade of the 1990s surprisingly well. As a consequence of apartheid policies, industry had been encouraged to adopt capital intensive strategies to minimize the demand for Black labour in urban areas. Manufacturing was especially hard hit by the economic downturn of the 1980s and the dismantling of protectionist instruments since 1994. Yet it has responded well to the opportunities offered by the increasing international integration of the economy and the trend decline in the value of the Rand. The sector has a broad technological base, skilled managers, and abundant but poorly skilled labour.

South Africa has sophisticated, liquid and deep financial markets, including active primary and secondary capital markets, money markets, the JSE Securities Exchange, a South African Futures Exchange, and the Bond Exchange of South Africa. Financial sector regulation is a responsibility of the Reserve Bank (for the banking sector) and of a Financial Services Board (for non-bank institutions). The banking sector is dominated by four major banks associated with major mining groups: ABSA Group, Standard Bank, First National Bank, and Nedcor. In addition, over a dozen foreign banks were active in the country in the 1990s (although many have since withdrawn). The insurance sector, like banking, has deregulated and demutualized. The South African Reserve Bank reports that the total assets of long-term insurers in 1999 amounted to some R665 billion. Other financial institutions include the Development Bank of Southern Africa, charged with promoting economic development and growth across the region, and the Land Bank, whose role is to provide retail and wholesale banking services to the commercial farming sector.

There are two key issues facing the financial sector today, the first of which is to ensure that the ramifications of further integration in the international economy, especially the removal of exchange controls, are well-managed. The second is responding to the financial services needs not just of the small minority of wealthy South Africans but those of the wider and poorer members of the society. Bank accounts and formal sector credit are expensive and difficult to obtain. Black South Africans often depend on informal networks or on co-operative rotating savings schemes (stokvels) to raise capital, and have often been at the mercy of unscrupulous elements in the micro-lending industry (which has come under Department of Trade and Industry regulation).

Tourism, Small Business and the Informal Sector

After decades of limited development in this sector, a consequence of apartheid, tourism has become the fastest growing sector of the South African economy, contributing almost 5 per cent of GDP and employing perhaps 7 per cent of the workforce. Because of the vast untapped potential that remains, it is hoped that tourism will continue to grow rapidly and may become South Africa's major employer within the next two decades. Of the more than 6 million foreign travellers to South Africa each year, the majority come from elsewhere in Africa. The tourism industry, however, has hitherto focused its marketing efforts on bigger spending tourists from the OECD zone.

Promotion of tourism has been most successful in the Western Cape, with the first eight of the country's top 20 tourist attractions lying in or around Cape Town. Other major attractions include the national game parks and private game reserves, and increasingly 'township tours' which aim to give visitors some experience of typical peri-urban living conditions and lifestyles. A major challenge lies in the need to harness the energies of the industry to the wider projects of job creation, poverty alleviation, sustainable rural livelihoods, and black economic empowerment.

Small, medium sized and micro-enterprises (SMMEs) are essential to both the economic development and the political stability of South Africa. Small businesses – those with less than 50 employees – account for more than half of those employed in the formal sector of the economy. Micro-enterprises, employing five or fewer people and often comprising single person operations, provide means of support for poorer families and communities. A variety of institutions play a role in aiding small and micro-enterprise. Most important among these is the Department of Trade and Industry, whose Enterprise Development chief directorate attempts to create an enabling environment for small business development. Ntsika Enterprise Promotion Agency and the National Manufacturing Advisory Centres, state agencies, provide support services to SMMEs, especially in the fields of management, marketing and business development capacity-building. Financial support for small business is available through the intermediaries of Khula Enterprise Finance which intervenes in the financial sector by providing credit guarantees as well as directly through its finance intermediaries. One key challenge in creating an enabling environment for small business has been the burden of regulation, including labour and taxation issues, that favours larger businesses over small, and makes movement from the informal to the formal sectors difficult.

Labour Relations

Public and private sector labour relations and collective bargaining processes have each improved markedly since 1994. A new legislative framework for labour relations was put in place in the mid-1990s through the *Labour Relations Act*, the *Basic Conditions of Employment Act*, and the *Employment Equity Act* (RSA 1995, 1997, 1998a). The labour relations and basic conditions legislation, both recently amended, have served to mitigate industrial relations conflict by creating new and effective institutional forums for dispute resolution. The employment equity legislation has sought to impose reporting and transformation requirements upon employers, to eliminate unfair discrimination and to provide redress for the effects of past discrimination in the workplace.

Three key institutions created to advance this ambitious policy agenda are the National Economic Development and Labour Council (NEDLAC), the Labour Court and the Council for Conciliation, Mediation and Arbitration (CCMA). NEDLAC provides a quasi-corporatist forum within which policy change impacting on producer interests can be debated and negotiated by representatives of organized business and labour (with a residual civil society representation). Business representation, however, continues to be institutionally fragmented in South Africa, with well over 200 registered employers' associations. The major conglomerates act severally to lobby government where particular interests are threatened, and chambers of business continue to be riven with divisions along regional and racial lines. A long-touted merger between the South African Chamber of Business (SACOB) and the National African Chamber of Commerce (NAFCOC) was put on ice yet again in 2002 after further divisions within and between the federations.

Labour is also fundamentally divided. Different trade unions have historically aligned themselves with opposing political parties. Industrial relations disputes have characteristically been shop floor driven and therefore not easily subject to binding union–business mediation. There are still around 500 trade unions, although rationalization and consolidation is underway. Perhaps three quarters of those in formal non-agricultural employment are unionized, with about a quarter of the economically active population members of trade unions.

The CCMA was empowered by the Labour Relations Act to mediate and resolve conflict between organized labour and business. Unlike its highly adversarial predecessors, it has achieved a settlement rate of around 70 per cent, thus reducing both industrial action and the burden on the courts of labour disputes. It seems that the relatively high degree of credibility the CCMA has established among both business people and representatives of organized labour has permitted it to play an important facilitatory role in reducing the impact of industrial relations conflict on the South African economy. The country lost around 1.4 million days to strike action and stay-aways in 2000 which contrasts quite sharply with the high-point of apartheid era conflict in 1987 when almost 6 million working days were lost to stoppages. While these achievements have been considerable, critics complain that the labour relations framework is partially responsible for the country's intractable unemployment problems, an issue we discuss under employment policy in Chapter 4.

Challenges

Of all the responsibilities of any government, achieving economic success is the burden for which it is most readily and unreasonably held to account by its citizens. The South African people are no exception. While citizens have remained sympathetic towards the government's difficulties in extending public services, the lack of employment opportunities has been a matter of profound and growing dissatisfaction for South Africans of all classes. The definition and measurement of levels of unemployment is highly controversial in South Africa, not least in the degree to which 'discouraged workers' should be excluded from the labour force (those able and willing to work). According to official definitions, the unemployment rate is more than 25 per cent. As we shall see in Chapter 4, a more appropriate 'expanded' definition places unemployment at closer to 40 per cent. According to official statistics, the number of economically active people in 1999 stood at around 13.5 million whereas the number of people employed (in both formal and informal sectors) was around 10.4 million. While the number of people employed is growing, so too is the number of those unemployed.

While 'jobless growth' would present a great long-term threat to social and political stability in South Africa, so too would low growth or no growth at all. Currently many business people perceive the economy to be locked into a relatively low trend growth rate of around 3 per cent, whereas most would view something in excess of 5 per cent as a prerequisite for a sustained reduction in unemployment. The slow growth is both caused by, and perpetuates, other problems such as low skills levels, poor education, and long-term unemployment. Contributory factors include HIV/AIDS, crime, corruption, and the emigration of skilled labour.

Unfortunately the challenge of raising the productive potential of the economy is a complex one. It demands energetic and sustained responses to a series of deep and intractable problems. Many of the barriers to faster growth – in the labour market, business and effective public investment – lie largely beyond government control. The country remains vulnerable to international financial and economic crises. Key problems – such as poor education and low skills levels – are profoundly difficult to correct within a generation, let alone within the decade or two across which the ANC can hope to extend its honeymoon with the voters. South Africa must make progress, moreover, in the face of HIV/AIDS, which will worsen skills shortages and place institutions under exceptional stress.

If the challenge of creating a growing economy, with stable prices, and the ability to absorb a growing working age population, is immense, South Africa also faces the parallel challenges of employment equity and black economic empowerment. The government is trying to transform the position of Black people and women in public and private sector employment. The policy has achieved success in creating a substantial middle class and cadre of Black professionals. At the same time, it has inevitably brought unintended consequences, including the 'poaching' of skilled Black workers and inflated wages. Employment equity legislation requires employers to devise equity strategies and to report on them annually to the Department of Labour, an approach that is hampered by problems of enforcement and 'indicator drift', as targets are met on paper without fundamental transformation of workplace relations.

In terms of ownership, the economy remains overwhelmingly dominated by White owners. Only a small proportion of JSE Securities Exchange shares, certainly less than 5 per cent, are held by non-Whites. Government and business alike recognize the potential long-term threat this state of affairs poses for the entrenchment of a stable and democratic society in South Africa. At the same time, the country's sovereign constitution – and the demands of international business – commit the government to respect property rights and to compensate fully for transfers of ownership.

The ANC has chosen to advance using a 'charter' system for each sector, through which key black empowerment targets are negotiated by key stakeholders. The most important and pathbreaking of these, the minerals charter, was negotiated in 2002 in association with controversial legislation to reshape regulation of the mining industry (RSA 2002). The negotiating process was fraught. A July 2002 draft of the mining empowerment charter, aiming for 51 per cent Black ownership of the industry within a decade, wiped billions of Rand off the value of mining stocks and jeopardized tens of billions of Rand of proposed investment in the industry amid fears of creeping nationalization. Stakeholders returned to negotiation, and emerged towards the end of the year with a more flexible and modest set of goals. The final charter seeks 15 per cent Black ownership within 5 years and 26 per cent in 10 years. In addition, a 'scorecard' system will allow mining houses to credit advances in procurement, employment equity (affirmative action), training, and worker savings plans as part of their overall empowerment records.

Some sectors have been more problematic than others. Fraught negotiations in the financial services industry, for example, contrast with rapid progress in the liquid fuels industry which is more than on track to meet its commitment to 25 per cent Black ownership in 10 years. In order to avoid the kind of uncertainty that so damaged the mining industry, and to ensure that investors are able to predict and quantify the implications of empowerment requirements, the ANC has promised a 'global transformation charter' to bring Black ownership and participation to more sustainable levels over clearly defined timeframes. While such exercises are inevitably painful for business, and also cannot move fast enough for the new generation of Black entrepreneurs, they represent a bold and innovative approach to reducing the uncertainty that would otherwise continue to surround Black economic empowerment.

4
Social Structure and Social Policy

In this chapter we explore the social structure of South Africa, and investigate the government's efforts to make the country less poverty-blighted and unequal. First, we place the society into comparative context, using international human development indicators to identify its relative developmental strengths and weaknesses. We go on to explore its key dimensions of relative and absolute disadvantage. Here we address the vexed conceptual and empirical issues that surround the analysis of inequality and social division. Just who is disadvantaged and why? Is South Africa essentially divided by race? Or is its inequality better explained in terms of class structure, rural deprivation, or gender oppression? In the second half of the chapter we appraise some key government strategies to improve the situation of the less advantaged: employment creation, social welfare, public service delivery, social infrastructure, and education policy.

Human Development in South Africa

South Africa is a middle-income developing country. Its Gross Domestic Product (GDP) per capita (adjusted for purchasing power parity for purposes of cross-country comparison) was $9401 in 2000. This places its income per head on a par with Poland ($9051), Chile ($9417), Uruguay ($9035), Costa Rica ($8650), or Mexico ($9023). In a ranking of countries by per capita income, South Africa would emerge in 51st place out of 173 countries (UNDP 2002).

Yet income per head tells us only a little about the quality of human experience in a society. To explore the ability of households and individuals to command the resources necessary for a 'reasonable' standard of living, it is necessary to use more complex multi-factor measures of poverty that include non-monetary elements in fields such as health and education. Perhaps the best known indicator, and that used most widely by policy makers to compare human well-being in different countries, is the United Nations Development Programme's 'Human Development Index' (HDI). The HDI measures a population's ability to develop its three 'most basic capabilities': to be able to lead a long and healthy life; to be knowledgeable; and to have access to the resources needed for a decent standard of living. Life expectancy is used as a proxy for the first capability, literacy and school and college enrolment for the second, and GDP per head for the third. The UNDP assesses a score for each proxy and the HDI is a simple average of the three dimension scores.

Such indices can only be broadly indicative. However, UNDP argues that the HDI helps to draw the attention of policy makers away from blunt economic statistics to focus instead on human outcomes, emphasizing that the overall lives of ordinary people should be the ultimate criteria for assessing the development of a country. To discover that two countries with the same level of income per person have very different human development outcomes, for example, can help to stimulate debate over which governments and policies are succeeding and why.

South Africa fares exceptionally poorly through the lens of HDI, especially in the light of its relatively high GDP. It is currently HDI ranked 107th out of 173 countries, with a human development index of 0.695. Countries with a similar GDP per head fare far better: Poland is ranked 37th, Chile 38th, Uruguay 40th, Costa Rica 43rd, and Mexico 54th. Brazil, with a per capita income of just $7625, comes in at 73, more than 30 places ahead of South Africa. In HDI terms, let us emphasize, South Africa is ranked on a par with countries that are far poorer in terms of income: Moldova ($2109 per capita), Jordan ($3966), Algeria ($5308), Vietnam ($1996), Egypt ($3635), or Mongolia ($1783). All told, South Africa lies some 56 places below the ranking one would expect for it judging purely on the basis of its income (UNDP 2002).

Why does a relatively affluent 'middle income' developing country like South Africa perform so badly in terms of HDI? One answer lies in the extreme inequality of income in the society, one of the highest in the world. Its income distribution, when examined on the basis of the Gini coefficient measure of inequality, is among the most unequal in the world (May 2000· 23). While on average it is not insubstantial, income is concentrated in a small and privileged segment of the population. Around 28 per cent of households earn less than R670 (Euro/$70) per month and almost half of the country's people live in poverty with access to neither money nor credit. Levels of unemployment – the key determinant of poverty in South Africa – are exceptionally high. Because unemployment has been growing over the past decade, on conservative official measures from 16 per cent in 1995 to around 30 per cent today, inequality is deepening. The share of the poorest half of households in national income was just 11.4 per cent in 1995, but it has fallen still further to 9.7 per cent today (Statistics South Africa 2002b).

A second explanation for South Africa's poor performance lies in its unequal public services. Access to such services is skewed, with the non-poor benefiting the most from public education, health, water, sanitation, and transport provision. Yet it is just such services that should contribute most to a healthy and knowledgeable population and compensate for inequality in the labour market. While availability of such services has been extended since 1994, poor households cannot pay the charges required to access them. One result is appalling deficiencies in health care, educational opportunities, and other public services in rural areas. This is reflected in provincial HDI measures, with predominantly rural provinces, such as Eastern Cape, Limpopo, and the North-West, scoring between 0.61 and 0.64 (on the government's own HDI measure) while more urban Gauteng and Western Cape achieve 0.76 and 0.77 respectively (Statistics South Africa 2002a: 95).

If income inequality and unequal public service provision explains much of South Africa's poor HDI performance, the country does badly even when compared to other highly unequal societies. Moreover, it is one of a very small number of countries whose HDI has slipped since 1995. For example, it has fallen behind Brazil, its historical twin in terms of entrenched inequality. A comparison between the UNDP appraisals of Brazil and South Africa is indeed instructive (see Table 4.1). The relatively impoverished Brazil achieves understandably lower scores for education (0.83) and GDP (0.72) than South Africa. Life expectancy in Brazil, however, in common with many other developing countries, has advanced impressively, from 59.5 in 1970–75 to 67.2 between 1995 and 2000, and 67.9 today. Infant mortality has been reduced from 95 per 1000 births to 32 today. Under five mortality has come down from 135 per 1000 to 38 per 1000. In South Africa, by contrast, infant mortality per 1000 live births has come down far less significantly from 80 (1970) to 55 (2000). Under-five mortality remains at 70 per 1000 (down from 115). Most importantly, the country faces the implications of an HIV/AIDS epidemic that will claim the lives of many millions over the next decade. Life expectancy at birth has remained almost constant, improving from 53.7 in 1970–75 to 56.7 in 1995–2000. South Africa's life expectancy index is 0.45, a reflection of the current life expectancy at birth in the country of only 52.1 years (UNDP 2002). It is expected to fall significantly as AIDS-related deaths begin to accelerate.

Table 4.1   South African and Brazilian HDI 1975–2000

Human development Year	HDI value RSA	HDI value Brazil
1975	0.649	0.644
1980	0.663	0.679
1985	0.683	0.692
1990	0.714	0.713
1995	0.724	0.737
2000	0.695	0.757

Source: Adapted from UNDP 2002.

Explaining Inequality

Once we set aside these exceptional effects of HIV/AIDS, there can be no single correct way to set out or explain the society's problems of inequality and human development. Segregation and apartheid created distinct racialized sets of economic opportunity and public service entitlement and their effects persist today. Inequality, however, is not simply a black and white issue. All societies exhibit inequality, regardless of racial politics, and South Africa's distinctive patterns of relative disadvantage therefore should not be attributed solely to a racialized policy history. Professional social scientists also seek to explain inequality in terms of rural–urban divides in a developing society, through the lenses of gender or intergenerational inequality, or even through the prism of disability. There is a gulf between those living in rural South Africa and urban South Africans, Black and White, who have potential access to the resources of the formal economy. Likewise, gender plays a significant role in disadvantage, with women disproportionately bearing the burden of poverty, disease, physical labour, and unemployment. Taking these factors together, for example, as many as 60 per cent of African rural women are unemployed, whereas the figure for urban African men is 38.5 per cent. HIV/AIDS has transformed the significance of disease and disability as a cause of poverty and inequality for those living with it and for their families and communities.

Social scientists, however, explain inequality primarily in terms of class. 'Class' here is not simply a way of referring to gradations of inequality between the wealthy, the middle class, the skilled workers, and the variously very disadvantaged. Rather, it refers to the ways in which the fundamental social relationships within a capitalist society – between capital and labour – generate differences in assets and opportunity. Class analysts argue that what appear to be divisions based on race are in fact founded at a more fundamental level upon class relations between the owners of the means of production and workers. The disadvantaged must sell their labour power to survive, and many are unable to secure anything other than pitiful remuneration or even to participate in the employment market at all. There is only a tiny small commercial farmer sector, and informal employment and small-scale entrepreneurial activity account for a very small part of the economy. South Africa is therefore a society in which people are overwhelmingly dependent on employment and wages.

Today the very poor are still overwhelmingly Black while Whites dominate the ownership of resources. However, White and Black no longer correspond to rich and poor. The poor, on a class interpretation, are poor not because they are Black, but rather because they live in households with very low income, either because none of its members have a job, or because whatever jobs they do have pay extremely low wages (Seekings and Nattrass forthcoming). In the 1950s, the income hierarchy was essentially racial, in the sense that Whites monopolized well paid employment and almost all Whites were reasonably remunerated. Indians and Coloureds occupied middling class locations, while Africans were at the bottom of a colour-coded employment hierarchy. Such an overlap between class and race was already eroding in the mid-1970s. While overall levels of inequality remained very high, rapid economic growth had already resulted in the development of a large African working class and a substantial middle class. While race was still overwhelmingly closely related to income, its effects were now mediated by other factors, such as education and access to new white-collar jobs. Racial division today has been further eroded by the deracialization of public policy, and by the removal of colour bars and other forms of employment discrimination. Greater equality of access to education, the removal of controls on the free movement of labour, and the ability of Black South Africans to enter into business and the professions, have contributed to the emergence of a Black middle class. There are new 'income gaps' in the society, between a multi-racial middle class and the rest of society, and between an African urban industrial working class and the African unemployed and very poor (Seekings and Nattrass forthcoming).

Yet the impact of the country's history on the racial composition of classes persists. In 1998 Thabo Mbeki famously described South Africa as a country divided into two nations, one Black and the other White. The White nation, he argued, 'is relatively prosperous, regardless of gender or geographic dispersal. It has ready access to a developed economic, physical, educational, communication, and other infrastructure'.

The second and larger nation is 'black and poor' and 'lives under conditions of grossly underdeveloped economic, physical, educational, communication and other infrastructure' (Hansard 29 May 1998, col. 3378; cited Seekings and Nattrass forthcoming). Viewed through this racial lens, the society is becoming more unequal. The household income of the 'average African household' has fallen by about a fifth since 1995. The average White household, by contrast, has seen a 15 per cent increase in income. The average White household now earns six times as much as the average Black one (Statistics South Africa 2002b).

Addressing Poverty and Inequality

Understanding the causes of poverty and inequality is a prerequisite for effectively reducing them. Analysis suggests that government policy directly targeted at racial redress, rural uplift, or gender equality cannot substantially reduce inequality alone, because the labour market is the crucial determinant of poverty and inequality. While race, gender, and rural development need their own policy responses, employment and labour market policy must be at the heart of government strategy.

Here we will consider four dimensions of government's response to its developmental crisis. Since unemployment and poorly remunerated work are key determinants of poverty, employment growth and the labour market will be our first area of concern. Second, the social welfare system, and particularly tax and benefit mechanisms, can be used to reduce inequality. Third, public services such as water, sanitation, health care, public transport, and the infrastructure necessary for economy development, have delivered benefits in kind which have combated inequality independently of employment. Fourth, the education system, which plays a special role in the perpetuation of inequality across generations, has received unique attention and resources. Finally, we address one key area of failure: gender has a special significance in South African patterns of disadvantage, but it has not figured prominently in government strategy.

Employment Policy

South Africa's unemployment crisis is relatively recent in origin. In the two decades after 1948, the state advantaged Whites and particularly Afrikaners by manipulating the labour market. Full employment, in combination with labour controls, limitations on the free movement and employment of non-Whites, and the use of colour bars at company level, contributed to high levels of disposable income for the White population. While the last decade has seen a move towards 'normality' in the labour market, with the removal of residual formal restrictions on employment opportunity for Black South Africans, the beneficial effects of this change have been mitigated by a radical change in overall levels of unemployment. In the 1950s, South Africa suffered from labour shortages because of the constraints on entry into the labour market constituted by 'influx control' at a time of rapid economic growth. By the 1970s, as the post-war economic boom came to an end, unemployment started to rise among the non-White population, reaching devastating levels, especially in rural South Africa, by the 1990s. While official statistics paint a grim enough picture of post-1994 unemployment almost doubling from 16 per cent in 1995 to 30 per cent in 2002, this official measure in fact understates a harsher reality, based as it is on a 'strict' definition of unemployment, which includes only those actively seeking work. A more appropriate 'expanded' definition would include 'discouraged' workseekers, who have no hope of finding employment where they live and cannot fund the transport and other costs associated with workseeking. Unemployment on such a definition was as high as 38.6 per cent in 1998, and not far short of 50 per cent for Africans (see Table 4.2).

Unemployment is an extremely serious problem, not merely because of its immediate impact in terms of poverty and inequality, but also

Table 4.2   Unemployment in South Africa, 1993 and 1998

	1993	1998
Unemployment (strict definition)		
African	15.7	33.4
Coloured	15.1	15.8
Indian	7.1	14.8
White	3.2	4.5
Total	12.7	26.1
Unemployment (expanded definition)		
African	37.7	47.6
Coloured	20.9	23.9
Indian	11.0	12.8
White	4.6	6.6
Total	29.4	38.6

Source: Adapted from Seekings and Nattrass forthcoming.

because it is the government's greatest failure in the eyes of the electorate. Yet the ANC has adopted a conservative approach to employment in its Growth, Employment, and Redistribution (GEAR) macroeconomic framework. This strategy is orthodox in that it views raised productivity as the primary route to higher employment, even if such productivity growth implies the loss of jobs in the short term. Whether the government is correct to take this view has been the subject of strenuous debate, particularly between the ANC and its alliance partners in the trade union movement. While public sector labour has been largely cushioned from the impacts of GEAR, the labour shedding process in the private sector (and to a degree in parastatals) has had considerable knock-on effects in an economy where one formal sector worker often supports very many family and community members.

The unemployment problem has deep roots in apartheid era maldistribution of access to assets and skills. According to the government's critics in the labour movement, however, the current crisis was precipitated by the opening of the economy to international trade over the past decade, and by the reduction in tariff protection for domestic producers, while ANC fiscal austerity simultaneously reduced government demand for goods and services. Such critics prescribe short-term job preservation and an expansionary fiscal policy to boost medium-term demand for labour. Job creation can only work, such critics claim, if the economy moves away from its dependence on capital intensive activities such as mining and mineral processing. The poor, moreover, require access to infrastructure, new skills, and finance so that their nascent businesses can grow and absorb labour. Labour-intensive activities, such as small-scale farming, and labour-absorbing activity, such as construction and public works, need to be promoted, and private investment on services, agriculture and construction incentivized.

A second set of critics, primarily in business, have a quite different diagnosis, focusing on unintended consequences of labour market regulation. The wage bargaining system is inflexible, encouraging industry level wage agreements that reduce overall employment levels. While the industrial relations framework mitigates conflict between employer and employee, the overall levels of regulation is a strong disincentive to employment-creation, especially for small- and medium-sized businesses. Regulation imposes heavy administrative and cost burdens and discourages job creation through excessive protection against dismissal. Shedding labour can be a protracted and difficult exercise. One consequence has been a proliferation of subcontracting arrangements through which businesses try to avoid compliance with employers' regulatory obligations.

Defenders of extensive regulation argue that because each formal sector worker supports many family and community dependants, the devastation caused by retrenchment is far greater than in an environment with high levels of employment and labour mobility. Regulation, it is true, advantages the currently employed over the currently unemployed. But employment relations in agriculture and domestic work have been extremely exploitative. Such trade-offs are inescapable, and there is no technical formula for balancing enhanced worker security and dignity against unemployment. In 2002, government reaffirmed its commitment to the current labour relations framework through a series of consolidatory amendments to post-1994 legislation. The right to strike was extended to striking over retrenchments, and companies are now obliged 'meaningfully' to consult before laying off workers. The loophole of subcontracting work to 'independent contractors' to evade payment of worker benefits and employer's tax contributions has been partially closed. The mandatory unemployment insurance fund has been extended to all employees. At the same time, the Minister of Labour has reiterated his determination to pursue an ambitious minimum wage strategy, setting lowest legal wages first for agricultural labour and then for domestic (household) work at between R600 and 800 ($60–80) per month, despite potentially substantial impacts on employment. Such commitments undoubtedly make more difficult the achievement of the conflicting goal of employment creation and so poverty and inequality alleviation.

Social Welfare Policy

For a middle-income developing country, South Africa has an ambitious social welfare system. The Department of Social Development (DSD) has a budget of a little over 8 per cent of government spending, administered largely at provincial level. The centrepiece of the social welfare system, and the key instrument of redistribution through the budget, is the national old age pension or 'aged person's grant'. This is distributed to almost 2 million South Africans and provides a bulwark against poverty in the poorest rural communities. The pension was deracialized in 1993, primarily through increases in the level of the formerly African pension. It has since been undergoing a managed erosion of about 1.5 per cent in real terms per annum. Other important transfers include the child support grant, which reaches a little under 800 000 beneficiaries. This grant reduces the intergenerational perpetuation of poverty, and has assumed an extra significance given the growth in orphans as a result of the

HIV/AIDS epidemic. It is currently proposed that the age of entitlement for the grant be raised from 7 to 14, and that the bureaucratic impediments to claiming the benefit – for example, the inability of the very poor and orphaned to secure citizenship papers in rural areas – should be addressed. The DSD also manages disabilities grants and foster care grants, with the former reaching some 50 000 South Africans and the latter more than ten times that number. In addition to these various social assistance transfers, the DSD runs a Poverty Relief Programme, which adopts a community-based approach to poverty alleviation. This programme has a primarily rural bias, and is aimed to provide short-term employment for women. The current focus of departmental activity is on preparing for the impact of HIV/AIDS, for those living with it and for their dependants and communities.

Over the past few years, a variety of campaigners in the trade union movement, churches, non-governmental organizations, universities and the official opposition Democratic Alliance have together clamoured for the government to institute a 'Basic Income Grant'. BIG would offer a guaranteed minimum income for all citizens, perhaps at the level of 100 Rand per month, and would be fully integrated into the taxation system. On the face of it an unlikely proposal in the context of a middle-income developing country, the grant's political credibility rests on South Africa's historical exceptionalism in its social welfare infrastructure, and especially on the effectiveness of the pensions system. However, such an expensive and complex extension of the welfare machinery is neither affordable nor institutionally feasible. The entire benefit system is already bedevilled by low take-up of entitlements by the very poor, and proponents of BIG have offered no convincing institutional mechanisms for improved delivery to those most in need. More likely is an intensification of efforts to increase take-up of existing grants, and perhaps a progressive reduction in the entitlement age for the aged person's grant.

Public Services and Social Infrastructure

Apartheid era public service provision heavily advantaged Whites, who received near-universal access to housing, electricity, water and sanitation, together with public transport, social welfare support and post-employment pensions. Non-Whites were deprived of basic public services, with non-urban Africans especially disadvantaged. The extension of public services to the population as a whole is a tremendous opportunity as well as a challenge. By providing services to those who

Table 4.3   Progress since 1994 on social infrastructure and services

Households having	% Oct. 1995	% Oct. 1999
access to clean water	78.5	83.4
electricity for lighting	63.5	69.8
phone/cellphone	29.1	34.9
public health service use	68.7	69.4
formal housing	65.8	69.9
flush/chemical toilet	56.9	55.8

Source: Adapted from South Africa Yearbook 2001/02 (GCIS 2002).

do not have them, the government can counteract the patterns of unemployment-driven inequality. While the government set out attractive sectoral policy frameworks, however, and came close to hitting tough delivery targets in house building, electrification, water supply, and health, critics have complained with increasing urgency that ordinary citizens are experiencing insufficient improvement in their living standards. Wider availability of services has been accompanied by rapidly escalating user fees and a backlog in payments as a result of the economic insecurity of households. Perhaps one in seven households have had their electricity disconnected at one time, and eight in ten of Telkom's new telephone lines have been disconnected (see Table 4.3).

Household Energy

Household energy provides a fascinating window onto the problems facing the government. Energy policy in South Africa has been dominated historically by commercial electricity use, with industry, mining, and business still accounting for some 60 per cent of consumption. Much of the economy is locked into a heavy dependence on cheap energy created in the 1970s and 1980s by over-investment in power generation. Mining and downstream industries have grown on the back of cheap energy, notably minerals processing, iron and steel, fertilizers, plastics, chemicals, and petroleum. The country's inherited over-capacity is due to end between 2007 and 2011, and the high 'energy intensity' of industry will make price increases costly for the economy.

Households account for 25 per cent of electricity consumption. Around seven in 10 households had access to electricity in 1999, up from 63.5 per cent in 1995, with around 3 million households electrified in the past decade. Yet while 70 per cent of households use electricity for lighting, only 55 per cent use it for cooking, and only 48 per cent for heating. Thus electricity is bringing the educational and leisure benefits of reading after dark and television (hitherto battery dependent). However, other benefits have not materialized. Citizens' health is still undermined by indoor coal burning. Death and disease from paraffin fires continue. Air quality still suffers from coal and wood fire emissions. Women still bear the burden of wood collection. Electrification has also not brought promised economic development, because low amperages and high prices preclude its use for refrigeration and power tools. Expensive electricity also brings extra user costs for schools and public institutions wishing to use it to support delivery and administrative improvements.

The parastatal Eskom has dominated generation, accounting for some 95 per cent of electricity production and transmission. Coal accounts for 90 per cent of production, gas less than 5 per cent, and nuclear and hydro-electric power for much of the residual. Electricity distribution is often chaotic. Eskom is also the biggest single distributor, but there are also 400 Municipal Electricity Departments involved, overseen by councils. Some 120 of these municipal suppliers have fewer than 1000 customers. This fragmentation results in high costs, low efficiency, limited scale economies, discrepancies in tariffs, and cross-subsidization of other municipal functions. Government strategy is to introduce competition in generation, restructure Eskom, and encourage private sector participation. Regional Electricity Distributors will replace ramshackle municipal systems. The key opponent of liberalization and marketization has been Eskom itself, which has scored many political successes through empowerment deals, ambitious delivery targets, and alignment with the government's Africa-oriented foreign policy. It made profits of more than 3 billion Rand in 2000 and claims to have connected perhaps 3 million people since 1990.

Numerous disconnections for non-payment, illegal reconnections, debt traps into which consumers have fallen, and politicized payment boycotts indicate widespread citizen discontent. The municipalities and small cities, meanwhile, are alarmed at plans to strip them of control of electricity reticulation. They fear the loss of credit control that consolidated billing brings, and they have unlikely allies in anti-privatization campaigners who oppose the growing use of markets and cost recovery in this sector. Government's flagship policy, a free basic electricity entitlement, was finally approved in late 2002, after years of pilot schemes. Previously proposed for up to 3 million households, the scheme will now apply to only 1 million of the poorest homes. Each will receive free up to 50 kilowatt hours of electricity – enough to provide lighting, radio, and other light services such as small stoves. It remains to be seen whether this scheme will provide practical and political relief for the government and for Eskom.

Water and Sanitation

Household water provides another window onto the challenge of delivering mass public services for the first time. South Africa's water affairs policy was until 1994 driven by supply side and water resource management issues. The Department of Water Affairs and Forestry (DWAF) emphasized river basin, dam and reservoir management, and bulk supply routing. Commercial agriculture and forestry accounted for about half of water use, with mining, manufacturing, and power responsible for around a fifth. Domestic water supply had been dealt with by 16 water boards concerned mainly with White consumers, and there were severe limitations of supply to the majority Black population. The incoming government noted in 1994 that 12 million South Africans had no access to clean water and 21 million had inadequate access.

DWAF argues that 7 million new consumers have been supplied since 1994, and that the remaining backlogs will be eliminated within the next decade. Household surveys for 1999, however, do not fully support this rosy picture. Those having access to clean water piped, on site, via a communal tap, or by tanker, increased from 79 to just 83 per cent between 1995 and 1999 (Statistics South Africa 2001). Boreholes and rainwater tanks accounted for 4.7 per cent of use, while 11.8 per cent of consumers still resorted to streams, rivers, and dams. Chemical or flush toilets were available to just 55.8 per cent. Child mortality has remained at alarmingly high levels in rural South Africa, and recent outbreaks of cholera indicate that the impressive water and sanitation policy is failing to advance with sufficient speed.

DWAF has wrestled energetically with constitutional and institutional obstacles to delivery. The 1996 Constitution allocated responsibility for water to central government, with the national department's role to build but not sustain or operate infrastructure. DWAF currently provides funds for infrastructure but implements through water boards, municipalities, NGOs or private partners. It ensures maintenance arrangements are robust, agrees projects with provinces and localities, builds the capacity of local government as an implementing agent, and manages its nascent 'universal' system of 'water providers'. Its strategy presupposes the central role of local government with the assistance of water boards, but in practice depends heavily on NGOs and private companies. The Community Water Supply and Sanitation Programme (CWSSP) claims to have supplied 2.9 million people between 1994 and 1999, while also building developmental capacity of municipalities. A municipal infrastructure framework (MIF) integrates water, sanitation, roads, drains, and electricity, while a Build, Operate, Train and Transfer (BoTT) protocol guides relations with the private sector. Complex tenders include local labour and gender requirements, and relevant provisions for training and the development of a 'payment culture'. Statutory Water Boards, established under the Water Services Act of 1997, are enjoined to assist local government, manage resources, facilitate cost effective delivery, monitor standards, provide bulk supplies, and transport and treat sewerage.

Further success is hampered by the slow pace of change among water boards, and limited municipal capacity, which has required transfer of responsibility to public–private partnerships or NGOs. Each of these agents has been widely criticized for project failure, usually traceable to very low consumption. New water infrastructure carries high fixed costs so rural users pay more despite their poverty. Poor consumers unsurprisingly may revert to traditional sources with all the health hazards and economic and gender disadvantages these bring. DWAF is having to subsidize projects heavily to make them viable, and communities have often allowed facilities (such as pumps) to fail or have failed to refuel them. Cost recovery (on the current 1300 schemes) may be at very low levels, and the intended health benefits have not fully materialized. Contaminated water, pipe failure, poor community maintenance, and limited community participation limit DWAF's determined advance.

One recent development has been the promise of a 'lifeline tariff' through which free basic supplies of water are to be supplied to poor consumers. Supporters of this programme claim it is the only way to reach the very poor who cannot afford the most minimal tariff. Yet critics argue that free water treats citizens as objects of aid rather than as partners, and that payment discourages accountability and so reliability of supplies. In the face of poverty, which drives the poor to unsafe sources of water, however, such a free basic water strategy is inescapable.

Housing

Housing has been another government priority. ANC housing policy first focused on a subsidy scheme that empowered individuals and communities to build property for the first time. Since 1994, the government has created more than a million 'housing opportunities' in this way. Housing subsidy programmes are now quite differentiated, and include rental subsidies, project-linked and individual subsidies, hostel subsidies, subsidies for people with disabilities or with HIV/AIDS, and a variety of others. Projected expenditure on housing and community development for 2003/4 is R9 040 400, or 2.6 per cent of the spending total.

The achievement pales, however, in the face of the current housing backlog of some 3 million units. Critics, moreover, claim that housing policy has created a very large number of poor quality homes in areas distant from potential work or economic opportunities. It has therefore entrenched apartheid's spatial patterns rather than challenging them, and substituted poor quality formal housing for often high quality informal housing. In addition, many new homeowners have proven unable to meet the heavy and sustained costs associated with home ownership, and they have been obliged (or incentivized) to sell to more wealthy purchasers, so undermining the intentions behind the housing subsidy. Housing policy has also been criticized for its failure to empower individuals and communities to build their own homes, and by so doing to develop their skills, capacities, and communities.

The government has responded positively to these perceived failings. In particular, there has been a new emphasis on quality in place of crude

---

Box 4.1   Land reform

Given the high profile of land transfers and seizures in Zimbabwe's current political and economic crises, government's low key approach to land reform has surprised many commentators. The South African programme has three prongs: restitution of land lost through racially discriminatory apartheid era laws; tenure reform to create legal coherence out of the diversity of inherited tenure forms; and land redistribution. While 70 000 restitution claims are being slowly processed, and tenure reform has advanced slowly but steadily since 1994, the redistribution strategy lacks urgency. Government aims to transfer 30 per cent of agricultural land to previously disadvantaged individuals and communities within the next 15 years, with beneficiaries receiving grants of between R20 000 and R100 000. Projected resources for agricultural support and development seem to be insufficient, however, and the programme is confined to land reform for agricultural development. Yet South Africa differs from its less developed neighbours in that contestation over land is primarily an urban or peri-urban phenomenon, with people looking not to farm but rather to make a home within striking distance of urban employment.

numerical targeting. Participation has also moved centre stage, with a People's Housing Process designed to promote a 'people-centred' approach through which communities are able to access the resources that will enable them to construct their own housing. An insistence on building houses has been replaced by a more flexible approach to the delivery of services such as water, sanitation, roads, and drainage, while leaving households and communities to build their own structures. Equally importantly, the former fixation with ownership as the central goal of housing policy has been replaced by an approach recognizing that renting is often the most appropriate strategy for low-income families and individuals.

Another major shift of emphasis has been a recognition of the significance of the spatial dimension to housing policy. Apartheid resulted in the creation of immense urban settlements at great distances from work opportunities, and there has been growing attention to land availability in or near to urban employment opportunities. Like similar states, South Africa is struggling to manage an urbanization process that brings ever-increasing demands for public services and land in urban areas.

An inability to mobilize private sector funds for low-income finance has plagued this sector since 1994. A National Housing Finance Corporation was founded in 1996 and continues to survive on government resources and returns on operations. It has not succeeded, however, in tempting the private sector to participate. The government is likely to pass legislation in 2003 to clamp down on practices such as 'redlining' – banks' defining of entire areas as unsuitable for loan finance – and to direct a greater proportion of finance towards low- and middle-income earners.

One important response to the multiple challenges of public service delivery, poverty alleviation, and urban development has been a new emphasis on the local sphere of government as the key developmental agent of the state. The country now has 'wall-to-wall' municipalities covering the entire land area, including six major metropolitan 'unicities' which are solely responsible for the administration of municipal government within their areas. Government has determined that municipalities will be at the centre of integrated development, and will be responsible for bringing together the whole range of public services and for stimulating economic development.

Education Policy

While initiatives in municipal infrastructure and public service delivery have been a major focus for innovation, public spending is still dominated

Table 4.4   Consolidated national and provincial spending on social services

Function	2002/03 as % of total spending	2002/03 in R millions
Social services (total)	47.6	144 160
Education	19.6	59 519
Health	11.2	33 981
Social security and welfare	13.5	40 873
Housing and community development	2.6	7 864
Other social services	0.6	1 924

Source: Adapted from National Treasury 2002.

by health, education, and social development (see Table 4.4). These sectors, in addition, have a major direct impact on alleviating inequality as well as involving both benefits in kind and direct government expenditure.

Education spending is by far the largest single item in the budget, accounting for one in every five Rand the government spends. The education system, moreover, has special significance as a mechanism through which inequality can be perpetuated or eroded. Poor quality or inappropriate education is also an obstacle to economic development and to the alleviation of poverty within a society. More equal access to an effective education system is one key way of addressing South Africa's various developmental and social challenges.

South Africa spends a lot on education for a middle-income developing country (a pattern not atypical in Anglophone Africa). Yet its education outcomes are in many respects unsatisfactory. The school system has been racially polarized and highly fragmented. Under apartheid, 'own affairs' departments managed Coloured and Indian education, while each of the Bantustans had its own department of education. Only in 1996 were 19 departments rationalized into a single education system. Whites were also heavily resourced at tertiary level, with English- and Afrikaans-medium universities striving to secure 'European' educational content and standards for this minority group. Non-White, and especially African, schools and colleges were starved of resources. In addition, a 'Bantu education' policy increased spending on mass education but deliberately aimed to constrain the skill levels of Africans so as to fit them better for their designated roles within the apartheid economy. Africans in any event were rarely able to complete schooling because of economic pressures.

Formal education today reaches the vast majority of children between the ages of seven and 15, with school attendance estimated at 94 per cent in this age group. Wage discrimination against rural Black teachers has been eliminated, and spending per pupil is far more equal than at any time in history. Teachers, however, remain under-qualified and facilities are uneven. Fees continue to discourage scholars from poor families, notwithstanding the formal obligation of schools to accept non-payers. The logistics of teaching material delivery are poor in rural areas, and patchy even in peri-urban schools close to major centres. School leaving certificate pass rates vary wildly – averaging 58 per cent in 2002 but with many schools having a very small number of passes (or even none at all). There have been many initiatives to improve school performance, including a controversial and poorly prepared shift to 'outcomes based education', a centrally defined curriculum, and efforts to improve the teaching of key skills such as mathematics. Currently, however, schools continue to perpetuate class disadvantage, and to provide unequal access to the skills that will determine success in the labour market.

Relatively few scholars complete secondary education and continue to tertiary institutions. Only 17 per cent of 2002 matriculants secured the 'exemptions' necessary for higher education admission. 288 000 people were attending university, 232 000 were at colleges, and 215 000 at a technikon (Statistics South Africa 2002a). The tertiary sector is undergoing upheaval. Apartheid's inheritance lives on in the privileges accorded to universities that historically serviced Whites, such as the country's two premier universities, Witwatersrand and University of Cape Town. Historically African universities, such as Fort Hare and the bantustan universities, are threatened with merger or dissolution. Universities everywhere are having to face the implications of technological and scientific advance and a rapidly changing labour market.

Women and Disadvantage

One further aspect of social structure that requires separate analysis is the nature of gender divisions within the society and the degree to which policy makers have addressed the challenge of redressing gender inequality. Gender equality is important not merely because human rights are premised on equal worth of all human beings but for the more pragmatic reason that greater gender equality is essential to the reduction of poverty. In South Africa, as in other countries, there are numerous impediments to women's exercise of their human rights and poverty impacts disproportionately on women. Their access to health services is poor. They are subject to sexual harassment and violence, have poor access to justice, and lack productive opportunities. They have primary responsibility for household maintenance and rural physical labour. A variety of traditions, cultures, and religions systematize and legitimize their exploitation.

There have been some gains in South Africa in recent decades through the efforts of women themselves. Whereas 25 years ago, brothers, uncles, or husbands mediated and controlled all aspects of women's entitlement to property and land, such unequivocal control is becoming far less common. Women, in consequence, have greater access to credit. Lacking education and facing discrimination in educational provision in most of the developing world, women in South Africa are also more likely than men to finish secondary school. Numerous women partici- pate in government at the highest level, including in parliament and the Cabinet. Yet the broader picture of disadvantage is clear. In South Africa, 18 million people, or less than half the population, fall below the official 'poverty line'. Yet, 71 per cent of African women live below the poverty line. Rural African unemployment is 45 per cent for men while for women it is perhaps 62 per cent (on the 'expanded' definition). Apartheid's gender effects included a migrant labour system that encouraged women-headed households. Women have been primarily responsible for household energy and water supplies, forcing them to engage in the extended and backbreaking labour of water and firewood collection. Land ownership and allocation, dominated by men, has systematically discriminated against them.

South African women (and their children) also experience exceptional levels of sexual and physical violence. Around 50 000 rapes are reported per annum, or more than one reported rape per hundred persons in any given year, the highest incidence in the world. Such figures, moreover, should be interpreted in the light of the extreme under-reporting of this crime, which some estimate at just 1 in 20 cases (Rape Crisis Cape Town 2002). Violence and rape are often characteristic of established relation- ships or marriages, and the rape of young children has become an increasingly widely recognized scourge in South African society.

Over the past decade, many governments, donors, and NGOs have adopted a 'gender mainstreaming' approach, with the aim of delivering rights to women and equality of opportunity. Such an approach seeks to place a gender perspective at the heart of any policy or programme so that, before a policy decision is taken, an analysis is made of its effects on women and men. This process initially requires gender analysis, data disaggregation by sex, and new project design, monitoring and impact assessment approaches. The roles, resources, and priorities of women need to be identified and explored, and basic equitable practices introduced. Clear equity commitments need to be made in each sector. Organizational capacity must be built and skilled staff trained to catalyse policy formation and commission relevant research.

South Africa has progressed only a very short way along the road towards gender mainstreaming. The Constitution guarantees formal equality before the law, and the ANC is committed to the development of a non-sexist South Africa. Employment equity and economic empowerment initiatives have been targeted at women and Black people, and many government projects – in departments such as Housing and Social Development – have been designed to reduce gender inequality. Mainstreaming, however, is as far away as ever. There remains a paucity of relevant data and research. Participatory methods are often poorly designed, and there is little gender analysis of the budgetary processes. There are few institutional levers through which policy can be influenced, by and for women. The Office on the Status of Women (based in the Presidency) is largely inactive. The Commission for Gender Equality, a statutory body, has placed land reform at top of its agenda, seeking strategies for access and security of tenure for rural women. The Commission, however, has been lambasted for its poor organization, limited capacity and funding (as well as suffering financial scandals). The Parliamentary Committee on Women has come under heavy political pressure from the Executive (including threats to its budget after attacks on Minister in the Presidency Essop Pahad at an August 2001 Gender Summit). The political leadership necessary to give substance to the vision of equality embodied in the constitution has not been manifested by the ANC.

Towards a More Equal Future?

There is no single correct way of mapping social structure or isolating the forms of inequality and disadvantage prevalent in a society. South Africa, as we have seen, is a society divided by race, class, employment status, location, and gender. While striving towards a more equal future, and building public services open to all, its government faces immense obstacles to success in reducing inequality. Indeed, like most other societies, South Africa faces the prospect of a deepening of some dimensions of its inequality. It is relatively easy to end comprehensive discrimination by race or by gender and to create opportunities for many women and Black people to advance within the society. It is far harder to transform the structure of opportunity itself and to reduce overall inequality of outcomes. Unemployment is currently the major force behind widening inequality in South Africa and there is no panacea for this problem. Wider economic forces reward those possessing scarce skills and assets while penalizing those who cannot add value in an increasingly knowledge-based economy, and governments everywhere have struggled to create instruments with which to respond.

5
Government

The South African state was a product of forced unification by the British imperial power in 1910. Unification required the suppression of African and Afrikaner societies, and the harnessing of their energies to a dynamic minerals economy. Across almost all of its short history, this state failed to command popular legitimacy. The 1910 *Act of Union* embodied a racial politics, cementing an alliance of interests between Boer and English-speaker by excluding non-Whites from political participation. After 1948, a state that had been an agent of imperial power was transformed into an instrument of Afrikaner nationalist advance. It was used to impose an increasingly brutal social engineering while launching Bantustans into quasi-independence and servicing Coloured and Indian South Africans through a labyrinthine bureaucracy of 'own affairs' departments. As domestic resistance to apartheid intensified, and as neighbouring countries secured liberation from colonial powers after 1974, the state increasingly became a dual instrument of internal oppression and external destabilization. By the mid-1980s, a powerful security establishment occupied the centre of the state surrounded by a fragmented machinery of mass service delivery.

The Making of a Constitutional Settlement

A constitution is forged in circumstances of intense and immediate pressure, in the face of a threat or even reality of civil war. Yet it is designed for the very long term, to endure for decades or even for centuries. South Africa is no exception in this respect. The interim constitution of 1993 – and so the 1996 final constitution it inevitably so decisively influenced – was designed to guide the society across future decades. Yet it was negotiated in a context of mass political upheaval and violence. Perhaps the most important outcome of all was the triumph of constitutional supremacy itself. South Africa now subscribes to the doctrine of 'constitutionalism', which specifies that citizens and officers of the state alike should be subject to the rules outlined in the constitution impartially applied. The South African constitution characterizes itself as 'the supreme law of the Republic' (RSA 1996: Section 2). All actions, individuals, and bodies are subject to its authority.

While an immediate context shaped the constitution's form, the inheritance of the 1910–94 period was also significant. Even through the period of security state dominance, the law was often a check on executive action, although the principle of 'parliamentary sovereignty' severely limited judicial authority. Cabinet government survived until an 'imperial presidency' emerged in the 1980s. In addition, parliament had a tradition of adversarial multi-party politics, albeit one stifled by NP dominance after 1948.

The negotiation period was marked by severe violence, especially in the area of what is today KwaZulu Natal where a low intensity civil war was conducted between the ANC and the traditionalist Inkatha Freedom Party for the support of Zulu-speakers. In addition, the White right, primarily Afrikaans-speakers, threatened military and civil insurrection. The military affiliates of anti-apartheid actors were meanwhile conducting high profile bombings and shootings. There was much debate about the kind of constitution best suited to such a 'deeply divided society' in which, for some, racial and ethnic division were entrenched and had to be accommodated within the constitution.

There were external pressures for liberal constitutionalism, from international powers and from domestic and international business. Many different models were mined for ideas. The German Federal system, in which the provinces enjoy considerable autonomy and co-operate with the federal government according to consensual principles, influenced some negotiators. The United States, from whom a bastardized Separation of Powers was borrowed, had a pervasive influence. The United Kingdom, whose unitary state was most closely related to the pre-existing South African state form, ultimately proved an exceptionally important model.

The ANC and the NP dominated interim constitution negotiations, while the IFP took brinkmanship to new extremes in its efforts to influence their outcome. The NP favoured a 'consociational' settlement, in which veto powers and proportional representation in the public service would be guaranteed to all designated ethnic groups. The IFP sought a high degree of autonomy for the province of KZN given the weakness of its support base elsewhere. The ANC, however, insisted upon an essentially unitary state, albeit one with certain guaranteed powers for the provinces and municipalities. A parliamentary system was chosen in preference to a presidential model, although elements of presidentialism and a partial separation of powers were included. The ambitious and carefully designed constitution, moreover, incorporated not just conventional liberal protections, but also certain socio-economic rights – to adequate housing, health care, water, and so on. The government was charged with responsibility for progressively realizing such entitlements.

The ANC's immensely impressive negotiating team, led by master strategist Cyril Ramaphosa, and backed by the liberation movement's power on the streets and in the factories, achieved most of its goals. South Africa emerged after 1994 with an Executive-centred and unitary state. Few powers are unambiguously devolved to provinces or local authorities, and the policy process is essentially internal to the national executive. There is a strong centre in which executive power is vested in the President, who is head of state and of government. The President is supposed to exercise power 'together with' cabinet members but at the same time he is responsible for their appointment. There is a clear hierarchy of President, Cabinet, and Deputy Ministers. Parliament's position, as we shall see, is essentially reactive, a position determined by political rather than constitutional factors.

The three 'powers of government' – legislation, execution, and adjudication – are each assigned to one branch of government at national

---

Box 5.1   Cyril Ramaphosa

Born in Soweto on 17 November 1952, Ramaphosa is the most gifted of an exceptional generation of ANC political leaders. As a law student and black consciousness activist at University of the North in the early 1970s, he was twice detained and held in solitary confinement for 11 months. After completing his legal studies in 1981, he joined labour federation the Council of Unions of South Africa, which charged him with launching the National Union of Mineworkers (NUM). By 1985 NUM had 100 000 members, and by 1987, with more than twice this number signed up, the union launched a major challenge to the minerals sector at the heart of the apartheid economy. Brought into the ANC-aligned Congress of South African Trade Unions (COSATU) that he helped to found, Ramaphosa's NUM was a backbone of mass protest against the Botha and de Klerk regimes. Ramaphosa led the ANC's constitutional negotiating team, and oversaw the drafting of the country's interim and final constitutions. Losing out to rival Thabo Mbeki for the Deputy Presidency, Ramaphosa was deployed by the ANC to the business sector where he has been a prominent proponent of black economic empowerment. Ramaphosa remains exceptionally popular with ANC members and a potential successor to Mbeki in 2009.

level: to parliament, president and cabinet, and the courts. In theory, such a 'separation of powers' avoids the concentration of too much power in any single institution. While the President has some legislative powers in assenting to laws and promulgating regulations, and some judicial authority in pardons, there are mechanisms that place his office under the influence of the other branches of government. The President is elected by National Assembly rather than directly by the people. He is vulnerable to impeachment (by two-thirds of the National Assembly) or to a vote of no confidence by the majority of the assembly, which triggers a general election. (As we shall see in the next chapter, such constitutional provisions do not guarantee that the power of the executive will be contained, especially where the ANC can effectively fuse executive and legislative power through its parliamentary caucus.) The parliament has two chambers with legislation passing through the National Assembly and a National Chamber of the Provinces. This second chamber of the bicameral parliament has 90 members, 10 from each of the provinces. The legislature approves the budget, and its portfolio committees oversee the activities of government departments.

Ministers are both individually and collectively responsible to the legislature. Collective responsibility is the doctrine that the Cabinet acts as a unit in determining policy, and ministers should therefore defend government positions rather than personal ones. If ministers wish to protest or oppose cabinet positions, they are obliged to resign. Individual responsibility of ministers is their obligation to inform parliament, explain executive behaviour, and even resign for failure in their area of responsibility. Neither form of accountability works well in practice in any contemporary setting and South Africa is no exception. Collective responsibility has limited public debate, and ministers have invariably shirked responsibility for mismanagement and maladministration in their departments.

The constitution also mandates a number of 'independent' offices which are designed to protect against illegal actions or abuses of power. These include an auditor-general's office, a public protector, a human rights commission, a commission for gender equality, a national language board, and an independent electoral commission. These bodies have performed unevenly, in part because of constricted funding by the government and in part because most appointees are senior members of the ANC and so cannot maintain sufficient distance or objectivity when it comes to government failure.

The system of provincial government contains certain additional checks on the centre. The notion of 'concurrent powers' is much employed in the constitution. In conjunction with the treatment of national, provincial, and municipal government as 'spheres' rather than 'tiers' of government, concurrency is intended to suggest a notional parity between them. In practice, the centre has been able to limit the autonomy of the provinces in South Africa, in part politically – for example, by forming alliances with the IFP in KZN and with the NP in Western Cape – but also by the imposition of internal ANC discipline. The municipalities, and especially the new 'unicities' of the major metropolitan areas, enjoy the greatest degree of autonomy from the centre, and have become fiefdoms that the executive finds it difficult to control.

Political Authority under the New Constitution

While some commentators have claimed it is 'federal' in character, others see South Africa's new political system as essentially 'unitary'. Yet there are no uncontested definitions of what these terms mean. At one extreme stand unitary states like France and the United Kingdom – or at least these states at an earlier stage of European integration – with a marked centralization of power at national level. At the other extreme stand the United States or Germany, highly decentralized polities, with most significant policy and political decisions taken, or at least shared, by sub-national units. Such decentralization, if it implies constitutional entrenchment of regional government with significant powers protected by the constitution, is usually treated as characteristic of a 'federal' system.

The country's constitutional negotiators explored a variety of federal and unitary systems, including the United States. In most respects a unique case, the original American states' constitutions predated the federal constitution of 1789, and contemporary citizen identity is primarily defined and shaped at state and city level. States have their own separation of powers between legislature, judiciary, and executive, and a dualistic legal system, with parallel federal and state jurisdictions, leaves the latter dominant in criminal and civil law. Legislative activism is embedded at state level, and both states and cities can raise revenues and so act with a considerable degree of autonomy. Almost all public policy is determined at state level or lower, with federal government setting structures of incentives or intervening to regulate interstate activity. Policing, transport, and social security are dominated by states, and even economic development and energy policy – national functions in almost all societies – are primarily state level activities in the United States.

The United States model illustrates many of the strengths and weaknesses of federalism. It protects against central tyranny, increases citizen participation, encourages innovation and learning, strengthens community identity and values, and can partially defuse deep conflicts of belief. At the same time, it is slow to respond to challenges and has cumbersome decision-making processes because of a plethora of levels – fatal flaws for a fragmented state like South Africa looking for coherent government.

Non-ANC constitution builders were also impressed by the moderated federalism of the Federal Republic of Germany whose 1949 'Basic Law' or Constitution was designed by the western allies to prevent the re-emergence of a powerful centralized state (such as Hitler's Third Reich). The Basic Law decentralizes power, encourages coalition government, and entrenches province ('land') autonomy. The constitution lists provincial prerogatives – education, mass media, and any other matter not explicitly preserved to federal government – and 'concurrent' competencies, including economic development, environmental policy, federal issues, defence, foreign trade, and macro-economic policy – a feature partially borrowed by South Africa's constitution. Provinces are represented in the upper house of the federal parliament (the Bundesrat), a 'conclave of states', which can block the lower house (or Bundestag). Bills changing the tax balance can be vetoed, and provinces have significant sources of tax revenue from indirect taxes and from a guaranteed share of the national government budget.

ANC negotiators were never very much taken with the strengths of the federal model. Within the ANC and its alliances, there were (and remain) social democrats and socialists attracted by the potential of central state intervention. Such intervention is especially attractive in developing countries or states going through periods of upheaval. The centre also helps to keep a society together, and to counteract potential centripetal tendencies – among them the ethnic tension feared by many commentators on post-colonial African politics. The likely desire of richer regions and provinces to increase their autonomy from the centre, and to retain their advantages in terms of standards of living and income, also made a unitary form attractive. The exile leadership of the ANC, furthermore, had a preference for centralization because of its fears that the ANC itself lacked cohesion domestically, and worried that provincial parties might be difficult for the centre to control.

The impact of the highly unitary United Kingdom system is evident in the new constitution. This state has historically possessed a dominant national executive, in which cabinet and a powerful prime minister create policy. A weak parliament exercises a reactive and policy-influencing role. Revenue raising and expenditure is monopolized by a strong and intrusive Treasury, and there have been (until recently) no regional elections or institutions and no real revenue raising powers at regional or local level. The conventional wisdom is that the Westminster system enjoys efficacy at the cost of representativeness, its strong and unchecked executive able to formulate policy, generate legislation, have it rubber stamped by parliament and implemented by national, regional, and local government agents. In a federal system like Germany, by contrast, consultation between national and provincial levels leaves all groups represented and all interests consulted. Policy makers – in part admittedly because of accompanying corporatism and coalition government – must advance by consensus. While highly representative, critics claim, the system is slow and muddled.

This appraisal misunderstands the relationship between consultation and efficacy, a significant factor in South Africa's governance today. While the United Kingdom's unitary structure makes the formulation and passage of legislation fast, the country has a history of policy failures. Its lack of consultation makes implementation less effective because people resist policies in which they have had no say and no stake. British governments have lost touch with local and regional issues, and this has now resulted in the weakening of the unitary state, the belated development of a regional tier of government for both developmental and democratic reasons, and the devolution of powers to Scotland and Wales. (The United Kingdom and Germany, of course, are now part of the new European Union multilevel system in which governance is distributed across provincial, national, and pan-European levels depending on a policy's nature and impacts.)

South Africa seems federal at first sight because of her sub-national provinces, each with its own legislature and executive. But the constitution promotes or at least sanctions a highly integrated system of government in which the national level can prevail over the provincial in both shared 'concurrent' responsibilities and supposedly 'exclusive' provincial competencies. The South African constitution embodies the language of German consociationalism but the reality of executive dominance in a unitary state.

The Executive

The executive is the dominant branch of government everywhere in the modern world, with the partial exception of the United States. It is responsible for executing the laws of parliament but it also contains the government, or the political executive, which is constituted in South

Africa by the President, the Cabinet, and the senior public service. So complex and interrelated are the activities of a modern administration that certain actors will be involved in the majority of significant policy initiatives in the country as a whole. The state's core includes the Cabinet, the Presidency (which contains a policy co-ordination unit, a secretariat, and a committee system), the Directors General who are the senior public servants in each department, the Treasury, and the intelligence and security services.

The executive has grown in power across the world since the modern South African state was created in 1910. The complexity and technical nature of policy has grown, the volume of legislation increased, and expert and interest group lobbies circle ever more frenetically around policy makers. In addition, the state has become ever more ambitious in policy co-ordination, trying to get public and private actors to work harmoniously together. Executive leadership in South Africa as elsewhere has been bolstered by the tumultuous history of the twentieth century. Economic interventionism has also played a role, as frameworks for budgeting, changing ownership structures, and creating regulatory systems each require specialist knowledge, secrecy, and credibility. Increasingly, private lobbying and the demands of executive-related international institutions have enhanced the leverage of the executive and undermined the legislature.

Corporatist relations between the executive, business and labour, and the emergence of welfare states have contributed to this trend. Foreign and defence policy have also played a major role in expanding the influence of the executive. Modern industrial war is driven by the executive branch and its relations with capital. It calls for concerted action and justifies central control and intervention. In addition it allows the raising of new taxes – which are never fully withdrawn after the cessation of conflict – and predisposes populations to listen and respond to national political leaders. In addition, the executive branch has responsibility for international agreements and institutions – in South Africa's case, dealing with environmental treaties, World Trade Organization regulations, the Southern African Development Community, the African Union, and the New Partnership for Africa's Development, among myriad others.

The South African constitution places the Cabinet towards the apex of this system of executive authority. Cabinet ministers, who give political direction to a million public servants, are appointed by the President. There are 29 departments. A Cabinet system is designed to manage government business by ensuring that all relevant parties are informed of, and contribute to, policy that impacts on their area of responsibility.

This is effected in Pretoria by a committee system based on 'clusters' of related departments. The key principle behind this system is that the departments in a cluster need to plan their activities together mindful of the impacts one department may have on others. Thus, criminal sentencing policy impacts on both Safety and Security (which manages the South African Police Service) and Correctional Services, which is responsible for prisons. In the Social Sector cluster, the implications of water, sanitation, electrification, and transport policy on the policy to build more rural clinics can be investigated by the relevant ministers and officials. The clusters – covering the economy, intergovernmental relations, the social sector, international relations, and justice – are serviced by officials in the Presidency.

In a cabinet system, decisions are taken where possible by interdepartmental agreement. Hard problems or turf wars are taken to cabinet committees, and intractable disputes between departments may be mediated by the Presidency. The committee system therefore relieves pressure on cabinet itself by defining points of disagreement and excluding irrelevant actors. Only if disputes are intractable, or a policy is highly significant politically or in terms of resource implications, is a dispute likely to make its way to Cabinet. This procedure gives recognition to the fact the Cabinet is not a good decision-making body, being overloaded, large, and unwieldy, and comprised of non-specialists in any particular policy area.

'The Executive power of the Republic vests in the President', according to Section 85 of the Constitution, but he is supposed to exercise this power jointly with cabinet. Yet, the 'clustering' system itself is managed by the Presidency, the most controversial institutional innovation of the Mbeki Presidency. The Presidency since 1999 has included a policy coordination unit vetting and monitoring policy clusters and a cabinet secretariat which services cabinet committees and ensures that the cabinet system operates smoothly.

At the apex of the Presidency is the President himself. At first sight he possesses a formidable array of powers. He is head of his party, head of state, and head of government. He appoints ministers and directors general, chairs the cabinet and determines its overall operation, chairs some cabinet committees and appoints the chairs of others, shapes international policy, and can adopt other policy areas and dominate them. He also appoints a vast range of public body members, giving him a huge realm of patronage running into thousands. In close liaison with the Government Communications and Information Service, he is well placed to manipulate the media. In addition, he can reduce the significance of full cabinet, terrorize his ministers with the threat of dismissal, and use outside advisers to double guess them while denying them any real opportunity to speak beyond their brief. He can also use alternate co-ordinating or dispute resolution procedures in the Treasury or within the ANC to override opposition.

Despite this appearance of overwhelming power, however, Presidents are tightly constrained by a variety of factors. Any President will lack the time, knowledge, and resources required to dominate to the extent permitted by the office. He relies on the knowledge resources of departments and ministers. In addition, he is politically vulnerable and must balance cabinet by faction, region, ethnicity, race, and gender, while respecting powerful colleagues with party constituencies, making use of a relatively small pool of genuine administrative talent, and accommodating members of alliance parties. Ministers, meanwhile, are scarcely political innocents themselves. Rather they are sometimes devious and sometimes charismatic, often media-savvy and opportunistic. Above all, however, it is events themselves – the unending stream of exhausting challenges that confront a president day in day out – and the loneliness of the office that will deplete the resources of any incumbent who tries to use his office to dominate the system of government.

The Legislature

In the early history of the doctrine of 'separation of powers' it was legislatures (and the 'tyranny of the majority' they threatened) that were the key opponent of 'balanced government'. But, over the course of the twentieth century, the power of legislatures has been eroded, primarily by the expansion of executive power. In developing countries, this executive dominance has often been accompanied by a more systematic subjugation of the judiciary and legislature to the executive and its leaders.

The National Assembly, like its United Kingdom equivalent the House of Commons, is sometimes described as a 'rubber stamp'. Liberation movement discipline under a powerful whips office, and the prevalence of majority government, combine to make its influence over policy tangential at best. Its members are unskilled in policy formation, too numerous, and lacking research and analytical resources. As the United Kingdom experience has shown, such amateurs can become the dupes or cronies of special interests and lobbyists, or lobby fodder for the whips. The National Assembly, like the Commons, has a limited and weak role in policy criticism. MPs do not really criticize policy at all, rather merely addressing a small number of implementation issues within select committees. Issue ventilation, moreover, is undermined by media and public inattention to the operations of the legislature. Finally, individual MPs have virtually no chance of introducing legislation and seeing it enacted.

There is a variety of reforms which might enhance the legislature's positive impact on the political and policy processes. First, the committee system might be restructured in order to create a committee career structure. MPs performing extended oversight committee functions could be given substantial pay increases, a major committee research secretariat could be created, and individual committee research budgets could be enhanced. Bolstered by powers to summon ministers, and a professionalization of standing committees to make them permanent, a rejuvenated committee system could provide a benign independent voice for better and more accountable government. Second, governing party dominance could be curtailed by reducing the intrusiveness of the whips and making their appointment a matter of legislator election rather than party imposition. Third, a culture of accountability might be enhanced by establishing a genuine link between MPs and constituencies. Fourth, there are strong grounds for radically reducing the number of MPs and providing them with a far higher level of resources and support in order that their conduct can be more effective. They would become better prepared for later ministerial roles. Their debate would be more informative and productive, and their policy-influencing activity would be more professional. As we shall see, however, the current ANC leadership is highly unlikely to embark upon such reforms.

The Judiciary

The third branch of government, the judiciary, is concerned with the application of the law. Laws are binding decisions that are made into rules and enforced by the state. In South Africa there is formal equality before the law: any law, in theory at least, is enforced equally on all regardless of position. Yet, the sources of law are not as clear cut as one might expect. Law originates primarily in the legislatures, including 'delegated' legislation in different spheres of government. The Constitution sets out a clear hierarchy, in which the Constitution is supreme, and below it lie national, then provincial, then municipal spheres. Law can also originate in statutes promulgated by the Executive or in 'delegated legislation'. In addition, the courts themselves make new law in their interpretation and application of existing laws.

'Common law', 'customary law', law established through the practice of 'traditional' courts, and Muslim family law, are also recognized in South Africa but are at the same time subject to the constitution (implying that ultimately they will move into line with it).

The application of law is always open to dispute. For example, the courts must adjudge whether a right has been infringed, a legal offence committed, what the nature of the infringement might be, what exactly the law says, and how precisely the law ought to be applied. The system through which such judgements are made in South Africa involves a number of different types of courts. Magistrates, appointed by the Minister of Justice, may serve in either district or (higher) regional courts, and deal with the overwhelming majority of cases. High Courts, appointed by the President concurrently with the Judicial Services Commission, deal with appeals from lower courts but also with many constitutional issues. The Supreme Court of Appeal is the highest court of appeal in all but constitutional matters.

The Constitutional Court is at the apex of the judiciary. South Africa enjoys constitutional supremacy. All laws and state actions must be consistent with the constitution (including its Bill of Rights). The Constitutional Court is a special and specialized court which interprets, protects, and enforces the Constitution. It is 'independent' in that it is appointed by the President and Cabinet in consultation with party leaders in the National Assembly, and the Judicial Services Commission submits a list from which these judges must be chosen. The JSC itself is a representative body comprising, in roughly equal measure, senior judges, parliamentarians, and acting lawyers. The key areas of jurisdiction of the court include the consistency of legislation with Constitution – if such legislation is referred to it by the President or a Premier – and disputes between spheres of government. The court also rules on the constitutionality of constitutional amendments (in which cases there are complex rules for different kinds of amendments) and on the consistency of government actions with the constitution (including the Bill of Rights).

One key issue that has arisen in South Africa with regard to the role of the constitutional court is whether the courts are genuinely 'independent', given that the executive dominates appointments. In addition, it is often asked whether they should be independent, given that the courts may obstruct the 'will of the people' as expressed in democratic elections. Some criticize the courts as unrepresentative, primarily made up of middle-class White males, and suggest that they should play no role whatsoever in making policy. Yet such a role is an inevitable consequence of the constitutional court's function of interpreting whether the executive is progressively realizing people's social and economic entitlements under the bill of rights to decent housing, health care, and education.

The National Sphere

We have so far looked at the state in terms of the division of labour and authority between its three branches. In the following sections, we look at the three 'spheres' of government, national, provincial, and local, through which the resources of the state are allocated (see Table 5.1). These spheres have been designed to create an integrated state after decades of apartheid-inspired division.

South Africa's segregated society was administered by a fragmented state. A multiplicity of institutions was required to support segregated public services. After 1948 this fragmentation worsened under the impact of petty apartheid legislation and growing imperatives of racial classification and residential segregation. 'High apartheid' took state fragmentation to new extremes, creating supposedly 'independent' sovereign states for each ethnic group. Those classified as Coloured or Indian under this system were accorded specific rights of residence, employment, and access to public services, so necessitating an elaborate bureaucratic nightmare of 'own affairs' departments in every sector.

National departments cover the range of activities we expect in any modern state. There are spending departments in health, housing, defence, and education; external affairs departments, in foreign affairs,

Table 5.1   National expenditure 2000–05

R million allocations	2000/01 outcome	2001/02 revised	2002/03 estimate	2003/04 estimate	2004/05 estimate
National government	73 142	87 317	96 106	103 307	109 911
Provincial government	108 904	121 206	132 420	142 844	152 363
Local government	5 576	6 552	6 552	8 580	10 235
Total	187 621	215 075	237 106	256 386	273 128
Debt interest	46 321	47 515	47 503	49 845	52 434
Contingency reserve		2 000	3 300	5 000	9 000
Main budget expenditure	233 942	262 590	287 909	311 231	334 561

Source: Adapted from *2002 Budget Review* (National Treasury 2002).

defence, and intelligence; and security and justice departments, including intelligence, safety and security, correctional services, justice and constitutional development, and home affairs. In addition, there are economic departments, such as departments of trade and industry, labour, and minerals and energy, and others concerned with intergovernmental relations and public sector reform. The key department is the Treasury which incorporates finance ministry and public expenditure control functions, and has launched an ambitious new financial management infrastructure for the public service. The Presidency is charged with reversing the historical legacy of apartheid fragmentation through policy co-ordination and cabinet committee innovations.

Provincial Government

The second sphere or tier of government is made up of nine provinces. These provinces are designed to be effective developmental but also political units, roles which sometimes come into conflict with each other. Provinces are responsible for many of the key spending and social transfer functions of government, in education, health, and social welfare. For this reason, provincial government expenditure amounted to more than 55 per cent of total expenditure in 2002–03 – although it is important to recognize that provinces spend this money under tight nationality imposed constraints. National government expenditure amounted to just 40 per cent of the total, with local government accounting for just 3.5 per cent of overall expenditure.

The functions of provinces are set out in some detail but with considerable ambiguity in the constitution. There are areas in which provinces are delegated exclusive responsibility, but primarily their function is in maintaining essential national standards, establishing minimal service standards, and securing essentially national goals of economic development and national security. Where there are conflicts between national and provincial spheres, the national almost always prevails. Provinces have legislative power over matters in schedules 4 and 5 of the constitution. Of these, the more significant schedule 4 lists 'concurrent' functions. 80 per cent of provincial budgets is spent on schedule 4 activities, which include the social sector broadly, and especially education, health, and welfare. Policy is primarily defined by national government and it is implemented by provinces (subject to national norms and standards). Provincial Members of Executive Council (MECs) shadow national departments, and portfolio committees in provincial legislatures oversee national decision-makers. Oversight rather than legislating has been the primary provincial parliamentary role, and provinces have a limited capacity to draft legislation. Hence it is national political imperatives and standards for delivery that have held sway, and a national budgetary framework and regulations on financial reporting and accountability that have defined the responsibilities of provincial officers.

Provinces have a Premier and an executive council of between 5 and 10 members. While their role is primarily to implement national rather than provincial legislation, they have scope for developing some provincial policy and for co-ordinating departments to best possible effect. Premiers are initially elected by the provincial legislature, but since 1997 the ANC's National Executive Committee has taken over this responsibility for ANC premiers. This change has uncoupled the positions of provincial ANC chair and provincial premier, creating an 'upward accountability' towards the centre.

MEC's portfolios are necessarily broad, given that there are at most ten of them, and the Premier and MECs are collectively and individually accountable to the legislature. Provinces have limited financial powers, with 96 per cent of their revenue coming from central government either through project funding or more normally according to an 'equitable share' formula that is designed to advance equity. The Financial and Fiscal Commission (a constitutionally established instrument) details the 'division of revenue' by sphere and then by province taking account of basic service provision and need, the capacity and efficiency of provinces and municipalities, provinces' developmental needs, economic disparities, national legislative obligations, and issues of predictability and stability. A Budget Council made up of Treasury and Finance MECs ultimately dominates the allocation process but it is obliged to take account of the FFC framework and advice in its decisions. There is very limited fiscal federalism with funding formulas determined and administered at the centre.

The constitution advances an ideal of 'co-operative governance' in which spheres must assist, support, and inform one another, should co-ordinate activities, adhere to agreements, and avoid using the law to settle disputes. The National Chamber of the Provinces (NCOP) acts on the basis of delegated votes from the provinces. In addition, there is an Intergovernmental Forum (IGF) comprising provincial premiers and national intergovernmental relations ministers, and a Technical Intergovernmental Committee (TIC) made up of Provincial Directors General (DGs), the DG in the Presidency, the FFC Chair, and the DGs of intergovernmental relations departments. There have been moves towards tighter control by Presidency with the IGF severely downgraded recently. Within the ANC leadership, in addition, there has been much debate about the future of provinces, with many believing that it is the municipalities – and their relationship to national government – that must lie at the centre of effective developmental governance.

Local Government

The third 'sphere' of government – the municipalities – has the most troubled history and faces the starkest challenges. Local government under apartheid enjoyed very little popular legitimacy. The quasi-states of the Bantustans were effectively an imposed third tier of government, unelected and unable to deliver public services. Widespread corruption and cronyism plagued them. Over much of South Africa there were simply no local government structures at all, the commercial farmers and White rural populations securing services directly from government agencies while the Black poor went unserviced. This troubled history has guaranteed the municipalities cannot easily fulfil the mass public service delivery role the government envisages for them. Problems with effectiveness and capacity of local institutions are likely to persist for a long time to come. The still limited legitimacy of local government, perhaps almost as much as economic insecurity, makes the persistence of service payment boycotts probable.

A broad framework for transformation of the local government sphere is now in place. There are three kinds of municipalities. The six 'Category A' municipalities – the new 'unicities' or metropolitan councils of Cape Town, Nelson Mandela Unicity (Port Elizabeth), Durban, Johannesburg, East Rand, and Tshwane (Pretoria) – enjoy exclusive legislative and executive authority over their areas. They are all characterized by high population density, extensive economic development, multiple business or industrial districts, and a complex and diverse economic base. Forty-seven Category C municipalities, or 'district councils', are a new creation, and represent an attempt to ensure 'wall-to-wall' local government, in place of the old patchy coverage of rural areas. Sometimes, they are based on old 'Regional Services Councils', which were late apartheid creations designed to deliver mass public services in poor rural areas. Brand new districts suffer from a wide variety of capacity and skills deficits. The rural areas they cover often suffer vast backlogs for even the most basic services. Such councils always include within them smaller Category B municipalities.

Category B or 'stand alone' councils share authority with a Category C municipality. There are 231 of them, although they still often cover vast areas, and they are in a mixed state of financial health. Some are small cities serving historically advantaged communities. These have latterly started to provide services to their poorer hinterlands, but usually not very much beyond. Critics of such councils argue they are perpetuating the advantages of historically White towns while doing too little to develop the historically disadvantaged communities that surround them. The majority of Category B municipalities are poor and indebted, and service only rural areas.

The responsibilities of municipalities are diverse and constantly growing. They deal with key infrastructural services such as the reticulation (final point delivery and user-charging) of water and electricity, and waste disposal services. It is in just such areas that the backlog of delivery is most pronounced. In addition, municipalities deal with social services and primary health care, and they are responsible for the application of a variety of laws passed by central government.

While the role of unicities is relatively clear – they enjoy unparallelled authority within their boundaries to develop and deliver services and to discharge their responsibilities – the division of labour between district and local councils is less clear cut. Many responsibilities have been moved to district level as a result of an amendment to the *Municipal Structures Act* of 13 October 2000. This amendment implies a gradual shift of staff, infrastructure, assets, liabilities, records, powers, and functions to districts, in order to permit them to perform a 'developmental role', including water and electricity reticulation and local economic development. A strong lobby within the ANC believes wealthy Category B municipalities have been dragging their feet over development and redistribution, and argues not merely for the further empowerment of districts but also for the transfer of provincial functions and resources to them. The Treasury and some departments are strongly opposed to this development, arguing that the existing capacity of functioning municipalities cannot be sacrificed and redistributed to unproven and often scarcely operational district councils. Category B authorities that are well-established and organized – such as Pietermaritzberg or East London – should instead be obliged to devote more of their energies and resources to improving public services in historically disadvantaged environs. This highly politicized dispute about the roles of different municipalities and the provinces is unlikely to be resolved rapidly.

Decision-making within municipalities follows a common system. There is mandatory election of councillors every five years, through proportional or mixed systems. The councillors elect a Speaker and either an Executive Mayor or an Executive Committee. Mayors are largely elected by party groups, in most parts of the country by the ANC. Within the ANC this process has been increasingly subject to centralization. Some office holders will be 'full-time' and so are paid – a matter that has become increasingly controversial as salaries have begun to grow without any clear relationship to skills or market-related considerations.

The notion of the Executive Mayor is sometimes proclaimed as an innovation, in the sense that it was not set out in the constitution, although it seems to be derivative of a similar (and unsuccessful) initiative in the United Kingdom. Executive mayors have very generally defined powers, primarily involving the monitoring of council management – which is overseen by the municipal manager, who is also the accounting officer of the municipality. An Executive Committee (which is not compulsory) co-ordinates council structures, makes recommendations, and deals with delegated material from the national and provincial levels. Ad hoc committees on specific issues may include non-councillors.

The functions of municipal executives vary quite widely depending on the nature of the authority in question. Primarily, they are responsible for delivering services, promoting local economic development, and creating a 'safe and healthy environment'. As an elected tier, they are expected to respond to community feedback and to add value to provincially determined policy by tailoring it to local conditions. Most challenging for many municipalities, they are formally charged with achieving financial viability, and this leaves them preoccupied on a day-to-day basis with trying to increasing cost-recovery through service payments, enforcing stringent new legislation on financial management, and attempting to keep control over staff budgets which make up the bulk of their expenditures.

The key issues facing municipalities over the next decade are resources and capacity. All suffer problems of arrears and some are close to technical insolvency. Many district councils are unable to meet statutory requirements for financial management, let alone to conform to the vast range of other guidelines imposed upon them by central government. At the same time, there remains fundamental conflict about both the role of municipalities – the degree to which they can aspire to be the motors of local economic development – and which types of structure should be given priority – districts, stand-alone councils, or perhaps provinces. For the unicities, there are additional debates about the role of cities in the age of 'globalization'. To what degree can and should the country's major urban centres aspire to join the class of 'world cities'?

Conclusions

The three spheres of government are settling down after a period of tumultuous change in both structures and functions. National government is developing according to a model of co-ordinated and coherent policy making through the influence of the Treasury and Presidency. Problems in intergovernmental relations are addressed by complex institutions operating within provinces and between provinces and national government. The municipalities are moving slowly towards a new role as developmental arms of the state, although currently they suffer from severe deficiencies in capacity and skills. The multiple impacts of regime change, institutional innovation and a new focus on mass service delivery will continue for some time to buffet all three spheres.

The constitution provides a uniquely South African solution to the problems of accountability and coherent policy making that have bedevilled all modern states. A powerful executive with mechanisms for intergovernmental co-ordination provides the possibility of coherent and integrated policy making, and a sustained drive towards development and growth. At the same time, legislature oversight and the entrenched constitutional authority of the judiciary provide mechanisms through which the abuse of such concentrated power can be averted. The bill of fundamental rights allows for redress where the executive is adjudged to have failed in its duty progressively to deliver on citizens' socioeconomic rights. The robustness of this system of accountability, however, and the degree to which other institutions and actors in society are willing or able to support it, remain open questions whose answers will be decided politically. Many authoritarian regimes have enjoyed enlightened constitutions, claimed to guarantee rights, maintained 'independent' judiciaries, and proclaimed adherence to rule of law. Ultimately any executive is held to account not by careful institutional design but by the efforts of a country's citizens using the full range of its political institutions and associations.

6
Political Life

The overarching issue in twentieth-century South African history was the exploitation and oppression of the majority of the country's people by its White minority. From 1948, a key secondary issue was the implications for the quality of political life of the increasingly authoritarian single party domination by the National Party. The shadow of apartheid continues to hang over the country's political life. While a democratic system has transformed the political class and popular participation, South African politics still turns around historically familiar issues. How can the vast racial imbalances of wealth and opportunity in the society be reduced? What will be the implications of one-party electoral dominance – today of the ANC – for the quality of the country's new democracy?

Electoral System

South Africa is a representative democracy with elections at national, provincial, and local levels. The 1996 constitution prescribes that two legislative bodies are to be elected at national level, the National Assembly and the National Council of Provinces (NCOP). In addition, it stipulates that the electoral system must be based on a common national voters' roll and that it must result 'in general' in proportional representation. The system chosen to fulfil this mandate for the national parliament was a highly proportional party list system, in which each party draws up closed and rank-ordered national and provincial lists of candidates for parliament. Elections are held every five years. The National Assembly has 400 members, 200 of whom are elected on national lists and 200 on the basis of provincial lists (with each province getting provincial list members in proportion to its population). The National Assembly elects the President who is the head of the executive branch of government, and who is responsible for governing in conjunction with the cabinet, which he appoints.

The nine provincial legislatures are elected on a separate but simultaneous ballot. Provincial legislatures in less populous provinces (such as

Northern Cape and Mpumalanga) have a relatively small number of members. Because the thresholds for winning a single seat are extremely low, the system encourages a very wide range of parties to compete both nationally and provincially. Local authorities are elected on a different cycle to national and provincial spheres. Elections in major unicities, especially in Durban and Cape Town, have been strongly contested and have the potential to produce surprises in future elections.

Members of national and provincial assemblies and municipalities lose their seats if they are ejected, or resign, from the party on whose list they were elected. (Government, however, enacted controversial and opportunistic 2002 legislation to enable windows of 'floor crossing' during which changes in party affiliation are possible. This allowed the ANC to secure a mid-term two-thirds majority in early 2003, and has threatened the viability of many smaller parties.) Critics complain that the electoral system is bedevilled by excessive centralization of party control, and provides for too little interaction between representatives and citizens. Some have argued for the introduction of a partially constituency-based system to reconcile participation with proportionality. Notwithstanding the commissioning of a major review of the electoral system by the Minister of Home Affairs, however, further changes to a system that well suits ANC party managers are highly unlikely.

The Electorate

The South African electorate is unusually sophisticated in both regional and global terms. The country's long history of rural–urban migrancy and political organization has left only a residual politics of the peasantry. Anti-apartheid campaigning created nationwide networks of cross-class and anti-ethnic political organization. Yet the analysis of voter behaviour until recently lagged behind this reality, with assumptions about race and ethnicity undermining political attitude and other social science research (Taylor and Orkin 1995). While Whites were treated as 'normal' objects of political enquiry, Black politics was viewed through the lenses of anthropology and as a mass phenomenon. Priority has been accorded to ethnic and racial categories and assumptions made about ethnic identity and social structure, often highly inappropriate to the social fluidity and geographical mobility of the country's individuals and households. Ethnicity (as opposed to income, age, gender or any other factor) has on occasion been the only analytic category employed in major surveys (e.g. Johnson and Schlemmer 1996). Understanding of the

South African electorate has been transformed by a new generation of professional research, notably at the Institute for Democracy in South Africa (Idasa 2002a,b,c), which for the first time allows study of the country's political and social attitudes in comparative context and over time. These studies provide insight into how citizens understand democracy, what they view as significant issues, and the degree to which they respect and trust political leaders and institutions.

In each of these three respects the picture is mixed. More than half of South Africans are generally positive about their system of government, including 46 per cent of Whites (up from just 12 per cent in 1995), and perhaps six in ten believe democracy is preferable to any other kind of government. However, a number of qualifications must be made to this rosy view. South Africans tend to view democracy instrumentally, with two-thirds of them seeing it as primarily a matter of delivering jobs, basic necessities, and education, rather than as being essentially a set of processes such as free elections, multi-party competition, or freedom of speech (Mattes 2002). Unlike electors in other African states, moreover, South Africans mostly view authoritarianism through the lenses of apartheid, rather than as a danger inherent in any political system (Idasa 2002a).

There is limited trust in the President (37 per cent), parliament (31 per cent), provincial government (28 per cent), and the defence force (32 per cent), and respect for the courts and police are also at low levels (Idasa 2002a). Perhaps most concerning, there has been growing coldness towards the governing ANC among many electors, with 42 per cent of those surveyed saying they would vote for the ANC in 2002 as against 56 per cent two years previously. ANC support in the key provinces of Gauteng, Western Cape and KZN had fallen to 33, 32, and 21 per cent (Idasa 2002c). Yet the ANC continues to lead in all nine provinces, with opposition parties failing to achieve credibility among those disenchanted with the ANC. Almost a third of voters in Western Cape and a quarter in KZN said they would not vote, and growing numbers refused to express an opinion. This creates the possibility that the ANC may continue to be elected by a growing proportion of a radically shrinking electorate.

Party Support and Political Parties

The key and inescapable fact of political life in South Africa is the degree to which the ANC dominates the county's electoral and political life. Conceiving itself as a 'liberation movement' rather than merely a political party, the ANC currently commands the allegiance of around two-thirds of voters in national elections. Through a series of alliances – with the trade union movement and South African Communist Party but also with key 'opposition' parties such as Inkatha Freedom Party and the New National Party – the ANC dominates the political terrain and seems set to do so for the foreseeable future (see Table 6.1).

The ANC emerged relatively recently as the pre-eminent force in South African politics, and as the almost unchallenged voice for its people's liberation. Founded in 1912 as the South African National Native Congress, the Congress has an extended history of internal factionalism, detachment from mass political organization, and political conservatism. In the 1920s and 1930s, these weaknesses lead to the marginalization of the Congress. In the period of economic growth and influx to the urban areas of the 1940s, however, the Youth League was established by a militant generation of leaders, including Anton Lembede, Oliver Tambo, Nelson Mandela, and Walter Sisulu, propagating a mild variant of pan-Africanist Black nationalism. Faced with National Party government from 1948, the ANC launched a series of defiance campaigns that for the first time brought it a position of national leadership, and provided a foundation for mass membership. The ANC joined with other anti-segregation forces in the 1950s to propagate the 'Freedom Charter', a quasi-socialist and non-racialist agenda which retained influence in later decades. Papering over divisions between Africanists and non-racialists, the charter did not, however, prevent the breakaway in 1959 of the Pan Africanist Congress (PAC) with its more activist Black nationalist agenda.

The political turmoil of the 1940s and 1950s culminated in the suppression of opposition activity from 1960. The ANC was declared illegal and commenced an underground armed struggle operating

Table 6.1   National election results 1994 and 1999 (%)

Party name	1994	1999
African National Congress	62.6	66.4
Democratic Party	1.7	9.6
Inkatha Freedom Party	10.5	8.6
(New) National Party	20.4	6.9
United Democratic Movement	—	3.4
African Christian Democratic Party	0.5	1.4
Freedom Front	2.2	0.8
Pan Africanist Congress	1.2	0.7
Other	0.9	2.2

Source: Adapted from Sadie 2001.

increasingly from neighbouring countries. The military wing of the ANC, 'spear of the nation' (Umkhonto we Sizwe or just mK), embarked on a long and ultimately fruitless campaign of espionage against a state with overwhelming military and intelligence superiority. Key ANC leaders, including Mandela, were jailed for treason in the 1963 Rivonia trial, and other ANC leaders moved into extended 'exile', in neighbouring countries, the United Kingdom, Scandinavia, the Soviet Union, East Germany, and Scandinavia, among others.

While its leadership was mostly imprisoned or in exile between the early 1960s and the early 1990s, organizations aligned with the ANC continued domestic opposition. The ANC aligned union federation, the Congress of South African Trade Unions (COSATU), combined industrial relations struggle with political activity in the later 1980s, and it has been part of a 'tripartite' alliance with the ANC and the South African Communist Party since 1994. In addition to the labour movement, a broader coalition called the United Democratic Front was formed in the 1980s to co-ordinate the anti-government activity of a variety of other civil society actors, including civic associations, churches, and non-governmental organizations.

The behaviour of the ANC as a political movement in government has been greatly influenced by three broad traditions: imprisonment, exile, and domestic civic and labour struggle. Beyond the famous older Robben Island generation, including Mandela, the experience of prison was diverse, with generational, gender and racial divides. The exile experience, if anything, was still more varied, with exiles engaging in all manner of activities – military, intelligence, or diplomatic – in a variety of sometimes authoritarian countries. Domestic struggle, likewise, took many forms, with certain key individuals formed by trade union activity while others were politically forged through community activism. The foot-soldiers of the final decade of struggle achieved a form of collective self-determination that was ultimately to collide with the hierarchical and authoritarian organizational traditions of exile and imprisonment.

Ideological diversity has also been marked, with many deeply religious activists co-operating with equally numerous communists and traditionalists. Communism was especially influential in the development of the ANC. The institutional embodiment of communism, the South African Communist Party, was formed in 1921, and went through periods of failed multi-racialism and Stalinization before adopting an unexceptional if slavish pro-Moscow profile after the Second World War. After its banning in 1950, it engaged actively in entryism of the ANC and became influential in the Congress movement's adoption of a non-racial position. Members of the SACP continued to consider themselves as a vanguard within the ANC, or as the most 'progressive' element within it, a self-conception that sometimes persists notwithstanding a repudiation of Leninist categories of cadre organization. The formal alliance between the ANC, COSATU, and the SACP served the ANC especially well in the run-up to, and early years of, the new democratic order. However, the SACP was very much affected by the demise of communism in the USSR, and this epochal event led to many doctrinal and political changes. Economic policy, in addition, has led to inevitable and growing tensions between the ANC and COSATU. The three movements' memberships, however, overlap almost completely and it is difficult to conceive of circumstances within which a conclusive rupture might occur. Currently, the SACP and many COSATU leaders have been complaining of the increasing dominance of Africanist and pro-capitalist elements within the leadership, and the stifling of debate by those close to the leader, Thabo Mbeki. The ANC's current leadership as a whole seems to possess no special attachment to representative democracy. The liberation movement's democratic tendencies co-exist with democratic centralist and hierarchical conceptions of legitimate authority. The struggle between these elements is unlikely to be decisively resolved in the foreseeable future.

Opposition Parties

Opposition politics has been the subject of much controversy. On the one hand, many observers believe that the country requires a robust opposition to counter ANC dominance and to provide the possibility of an alternative government. On the other hand, robust opposition seems to others to threaten the fragile stability and political co-operation that this new democracy requires. The Democratic Party (DP) has been the only consistent supporter of the first view, and it was rewarded in 1999 by the highest vote of any opposition party at 9.6 per cent, making it the 'official opposition'. The avowedly 'liberal' DP was formed in 1989 in a merger of four small centrist parties in the all White parliament. It served as official opposition to the NP from that year with a programme of non-racial democracy, a limited state, constitutional supremacy, and a market economy. It was trounced in the 1994 election by the NP under F W de Klerk which virtually monopolized the White vote, and secured additional support from Coloured South Africans.

Under the combative leadership of Tony Leon, a believer in robust opposition, the party campaigned in the 1999 election on a 'fight back' platform. Its relative success was secured largely at the expense of the NP, which lost both Afrikaans and English-speakers to the Democratic Party at this election. Confronted with the need to move beyond a purely White electoral base if it was to become a credible counterweight to the ANC, the DP embarked on a 'Democratic Alliance' with the 'New' National Party which it had roundly defeated at the polls. This strategy backfired on the DP when tensions between party leaderships at national level and within the Western Cape led to a split, with the National Party returning to an alliance with the ANC. The DA's strategy for moving beyond its White and Cape support base remains unclear and its national support at the start of 2003 stood at just one in 20 voters (Idasa 2002c).

The National Party, founded in 1914 as a vehicle for Afrikaner ethnic nationalism, was one of the twentieth century's most successful political movements. It governed without interruption between 1948 and 1994, in which period it elaborated and ultimately dismantled the system of apartheid. The party transformed the political landscape of South Africa, securing hegemony across the White electorate while catapulting Afrikaners to near income equality with English-speakers. Its performance since 1994 has been both unexpected and ironic. The NP gained credit with the ANC for its willingness to participate in negotiations and concede a relatively bloodless transfer of power, and to participate in the Government of National Unity (GNU) between 1994 and 1996.

After picking up a fifth of the vote in the 1994 election, the NP played a crucial role in convincing international markets and domestic business of the stability and fiscal rectitude of the incoming liberation movement. When it abandoned GNU for opposition in 1996, however, its supporters deserted in droves for the more confrontational opposition of the Democratic Party (DP). The NP was reduced to a regional party in the Western Cape, deriving most of its support from the Coloured South Africans it had oppressed in the apartheid era. Picking up the pieces after this reversal, its new leader Marthinus van Skalkwyk has re-branded the party (rather unconvincingly) as the 'New' National Party (NNP) and embarked upon opportunistic alliances, first with the DP, and now with the ANC. After the collapse of its alliance with the DP, the NNP secured an agreement with the ANC to form an alliance in the Western Cape to wrestle control of the prize of Cape Town from the DP. The future of this alliance, however, is open to question. Many in the ANC are deeply uncomfortable sharing even the illusion of power with the ANC's historic adversary and the creator of apartheid. More importantly, it is unclear how the electorate will respond to the 'desertion' of councillors to an alliance with the ANC that many of those electors were desperate to reject. Support for the party currently stands at around 3 per cent, and perhaps at 10 per cent in the Western Cape (Idasa 2002c).

The Inkatha Freedom Party (IFP) is South Africa's most prominent vehicle for ethnic mobilization but also the personal instrument of its leader Mangosuthu Buthelezi. It campaigns on a Zulu nationalist platform, and its electorate is drawn predominantly from the poorer population of the most populous province, KwaZulu Natal. The IFP's support base has been inexorably eroded by the ANC as the Zulu-speaking population of the province becomes increasingly urbanized. The key significance of the movement has been its challenge to ANC provincial hegemony, and its ability to use violence as a veto on political change in the province. The IFP continues participates in national government, with Buthelezi the Home Affairs minister. However, he has been willing to enter into alliances with the DP at provincial level in order to obstruct an ANC take-over of the provincial government.

Two smaller parties, the Pan Africanist Congress (PAC) and the United Democratic Movement (UDM), have only 1 per cent support each in a recent poll (Idasa 2002c). They are nonetheless significant as the major Black-led opposition to the ANC in a country in which historically White parties' attacks on government have been trivialized as racially motivated. The UDM, created by the former homeland leader Bantu Holomisa in a short-lived alliance with former NP constitutional negotiator Roelf Meyer, stands on a classical anti-corruption and pro-delivery platform. Its limited support base is concentrated in the Eastern Cape and depends on the charismatic authority of Holomisa who was expelled from the ANC for levelling allegations of corruption against a cabinet Minister. The PAC, long-standing rival to the ANC but bedevilled by infighting and a lack of political professionalism, has seen its share of the vote collapse perhaps beyond recovery. Both the UDM and the PAC have been hit especially hard by 'floor-crossing' legislation which has allowed the ANC to poach electorally vulnerable members of smaller parties by promising them a high placing in the ANC's almost impregnable party lists.

Interest and Pressure Groups

A pressure or interest group is an association of people with shared goals or values which tries to influence the policy process. It is distinct from a party in that it does not seek to govern, has a narrower membership, typically focuses on a number of specific issues, and is unelected by the electorate and so not accountable to it. Some analysts have viewed South Africa as a quasi-'corporatist' state, in which the interests of labour and business have been formally incorporated into the policy making process. Others have stressed the state's pluralist aspects, and particularly the prominent role of civil society organizations in the struggle for democracy. A longer standing tradition focuses on the power of business, and especially the mining sector, in setting the country's policy agenda.

In South Africa, producer groups – such as trade unions and business federations – suffer from organizational fragmentation. The ANC has created a quasi-corporatist bargaining forum called the National Economic Development and Labour Council (NEDLAC) which is designed to bring business and labour together in consultation. NEDLAC, however, has been bypassed by powerful business and labour interests. The most powerful union federation, COSATU, has used its relationship with the ANC to secure gains in industrial relations legislation and public sector job protection. Where conflict has escalated between COSATU and the government, notably over privatization policy, the union federation has resorted to campaigns, strikes, and political mobilization within the alliance, rather than depending on NEDLAC structures.

Business has also bypassed corporatist structures. The South African economy has been dominated historically by a small number of resources groups with operations across mining, manufacturing, services, and the financial sector. Each has the political weight to demand an audience with government on its own terms. President Mbeki is extremely sensitive to the demands of domestic and international big business, and has opened new institutional channels to the presidency for lobbies such as the National Business Initiative and the South African Foundation. Smaller business groups, still prone to factionalism and paralysed for a decade by racial divisions between the South African Chamber of Business (SACOB) and National African Chamber of Commerce (NAFCOC), have been far less effective players. (Professional associations, protected by their monopoly on skills, also suffer persistent racial tensions. Lawyers, for example, continue to be divided between the (primarily White) Law Society of South Africa and the Black Lawyers Association.)

Relations between business and government have not always been easy. Many in government, emotionally or ideologically aligned with labour, are suspicious of the intentions of big business. Conflict over 'Black economic empowerment', the process by which the non-White population can secure more proportional ownership of the country's productive assets, has been simmering. Measuring the extent of Black ownership is controversial, in part because it involves identifying complex 'empowerment vehicles' whose ultimate ownership is unknown, and uncovering the degree to which Black South Africans are owners by virtue of their contributions to insurance and pension funds. Recent estimates of Black ownership lie between 2 and 10 per cent, with the former the more realistic assessment.

Non-sectional associations, proclaiming universal goals or declaring that they act on behalf of humanity as a whole, are weaker than their sectional cousins. However, South Africa has historically possessed an unusually vibrant civil society, with very large numbers of active non-governmental organizations (NGOs), churches, and campaign groups. Before 1994, the vast majority of these groups were aligned with the ANC, or at least strongly opposed to apartheid. The post-1994 found many of them struggling to retain influence in a less indulgent donor environment.

Voluntary campaign groups became rare, suffering from shortages of resources and access to the media and an unwillingness to confront the ANC movement their activists once championed. The past three years, however, have seen a transformation in post-1994 political campaigning. Networks of community-based mass movements have formed. Campaign groups, often strongly opposed to government policy and practice, have taken to the streets in defiance of erstwhile ANC allies, who now characterize them as ultra-leftists and the enemies of the liberation movement. For some commentators, we are witnessing the triumphant rebirth of oppositional civil society after a decade of transitional quiescence. For others the new social movements are led by anti-democratic and unrealistic ideologues, fighting against the international businesses and systematic government programmes that offer the best hope for the disadvantaged masses on whose behalf they presume to speak.

The new campaign networks mostly began as issue-based movements. The most visible and long established of the campaign groups has been the Treatment Action Campaign (TAC), campaigning effectively and creatively since 1988 against the government's position on the treatment and support of those living with HIV/AIDS, although with a markedly higher profile since 2000. The TAC's primary public focus has been on the public provision of anti-retroviral treatments to prevent the transmission of HIV from pregnant mother to child. It has used a variety of campaigning instruments: public protest, constitutional challenges, and from 2003, a mass programme of non-violent civil disobedience. The far larger (200 000 member) National Association of People Living with HIV/AIDS (NAPWA) has pursued the goals of de-stigmatization and prevention, while until recently taking a highly conciliatory line towards government.

Another established group, the National Land Committee (NLC), was established in 1987 through the countrywide affiliation of land reform organizations. Recently it has become a more vehement (and perhaps less coherent) critic of government policy on rural and urban land redistribution. A far more fluid and anti-hierarchical mass movement closely aligned with the NLC, the Landless People's Movement, has since 2001 taken a stronger position on farm labourers' rights and the need for a more ambitious land reform strategy.

Soweto Electricity Crisis Committee (SECC), established in 2000 to protest against electricity disconnections for payment defaulters by the parastatal Eskom, conducts illegal reconnections through its 'Operation Khanyisa' (light). It has recently diversified into protest against water cutoffs and the eviction of rent or bond (housing loan) defaulters. SECC appears to have among its executive leadership both community activists, union activists, and leftist intellectuals and it has relationships with wider anti-privatization networks. Similar umbrella organizations exist in major urban areas across South Africa. In Cape Town, for example, a vigorous Anti-Eviction Campaign which emerged in 2000 around the issue of township bond-default evictions today includes water and electricity campaigning in its portfolio. The most militant and ambitious leftist grouping, formed in 2000, is the Anti-Privatization Forum (APF). The APF is dominated by organized labour and by members of the radical left disenchanted with the ANC's priorities and performance in power. Organized initially against privatization and public–private partnerships for the provision of municipal infrastructure, the APF has become an umbrella for more than a dozen other campaign groups, including SECC.

The significance of such mass protest movements is still unclear, although they have evidently aroused considerable ire within the ANC. A lively debate continues within the liberation movement about the proper role of pressure groups. Against the backdrop of increasing irritation on the part of the government with anti-privatization, landless people's, and HIV/AIDS campaigns, government has sought to increase central control over donor funds to bring the NGO sector into line with its strategic priorities. Some ANC leaders are growing increasingly sceptical that pressure group activity is conducive to democracy (while themselves being accused by radicals of being in the pockets of business interests). Favouring integrated executive-driven policy, they do not welcome opposition to specific parts of a manifesto or increased responsiveness of the political system to minorities. Many liberation movement leaders habitually reiterate the centrality of majority rule to democracy, and stress the dangers of allowing undue minority influence on policy. Sectional interest groups, they claim, may impose very heavy costs on non-members through their protest actions (and especially through strikes). Well-organized and well-resourced groups may achieve disproportionate power. New social movements and campaigning NGOs, ANC leaders often darkly remark, are the recipients of foreign funding. On occasion, the same critics (and notably, on one very public occasion in 2003, the Health Minister Manto Tshabalala-Msimang) have referred to the disproportionate influence of White intellectuals and activists within new social movements and campaign groups. The weak and the poor who support the ANC in elections, on this view, cannot organize as effectively as the White or ultra-leftist leaders of these atypical and 'unpatriotic' social movements.

More acceptable to the ANC has been the notion that civil society actors can provide the government with vital information and knowledge and act as partners in delivery of public services. In particular, such partners can inform the government about the issues that trouble particular sections of the community, highlight implementation failures, and provide suggestions for policy improvement. This role is once again significant in South Africa where government capacity is stretched, and the government is showing new willingness to work on 'delivery issues' with NGO partners. Some NGOs perform valuable knowledge generating and political oversight functions, with Institute for Democracy in South Africa (IDASA) and Electoral Institute of South Africa (EISA) especially noteworthy in this regard. Such organizations have walked a fine line in their relationships with a government that has not been indulgent of critics. Other NGOs have been drawn into extended consulting for government on policy, and into acting as its implementing agents.

South Africa has yet to reach any national consensus on the proper role of voluntary associations – a debate that is part of the political process in any democracy. South Africans' sometimes moralizing approach to politics does not leave space for the pluralist notion that individuals acting together, self-interestedly, and in furtherance of their particular goals, can unintentionally create better outcomes for all than well-meaning groups with the common good as their goal.

The Implications of One-Party Dominance

The central focus of political analysis in South Africa today is on the future of its democracy. Comparative social scientists claim that the performance of new democracies elsewhere can shed light on South

Africa's prospects, and on the conditions it must meet if its democracy is to be 'consolidated'. Yet using comparative political analysis to predict or improve the future has not proven easy. It is difficult at the best of times to generalize about complex processes on the basis of a small number of cases, but well-nigh impossible when the comparative framework is based on wholly inappropriate categories. Models used to understand democracy in Africa have been shaped by data originating in quite different circumstances. The southern European experiences of 1974–76, influenced by individuals' deaths, colonial wars, and generational change, and spilling over into Latin American liberalization, shattered previously deterministic explanatory frameworks. The rapid and bunched east and central European transitions, with their 'contagion effects' and external precipitation in Moscow, forced a further productive intellectual reconfiguration. African 'democratization', by contrast, generated no fundamental theoretical innovation, its distinct causal dynamic of post-Cold War external engineering and imposed good governance instead treated as anomalous. The fallacy advanced by democracy promotion and protection experts everywhere – if specific features of enduring democracies are absent in a particular country, then, they must be introduced forthwith – is least credible in Africa.

Systematic cross-national analysis has identified broad sets of factors – economic growth, stable political institutions, and an appropriate political culture – that have elsewhere and in the past been associated with measures of democratic persistence. Yet each of these sets of factors in South Africa, according to one lucid analysis, presents a 'paradox' rather than any clear basis for judgement (Mattes 2002). Macro-economic stability sits uneasily alongside low investment and extreme unemployment; state-of-the-art mechanisms of accountability are vitiated by one-party dominance; and a diverse civil society accompanies uneven commitment to democracy and participation. Domestic authors more commonly treat 'consolidation' as little more than a semantic issue, believing that the key formal attributes of liberal polyarchy are entrenched for the next decade or more, while ANC electoral domination precludes any transfer of power. The focus of local investigation has therefore been on the quality of political life under a period of extended 'one-party dominance', and on the implications of such dominance for the longer-term future of the polity.

The common expectation of protracted ANC electoral dominance is partly extrapolated from the tripartite ANC–SACP–COSATU alliance's two previous near two-thirds majorities in national elections. Even a recently touted 'coalition of hope' between four opposition parties – the

IFP, the DP, the UDM, and the PAC – could hope on current projections to muster only a third of the vote in the 2004 parliamentary elections. Yet even this seems fanciful, in the light of the recent ignominious collapse of a more modest alliance between the DP and the NNP, which saw the latter scuttling back to the ANC to seek peace on extremely unfavourable terms. Given the obstacles to opposition coalition-building, a split in the ruling alliance and the desertion of its followers *en masse* are necessary conditions for the emergence of an alternative government. While I shall argue that this possibility cannot be discounted, the ANC has proven adroit at enticing opposition elements into its circle of alliances and holding them there.

South Africa's constitutional framework translates electoral dominance very directly into a preponderance of political power in the executive and legislature. The 1996 constitution, as we have seen, perpetuates the country's traditionally centralized system of executive authority. Despite certain 'concurrent powers' and a language of 'co-operative governance', the state is essentially unitary, with almost no revenue raising or legislative capacity delegated to the provinces. Parliament is a bloated and largely reactive policy-influencing legislature on the Westminster model, but with strict party discipline reinforced by a party-list proportional system permitting easy 'redeployment' of disloyal members.

The ANC's overwhelming political power under this system has been greeted both positively and negatively. On the one hand, many analysts consider that only an extended period of political stability can establish the preconditions for the longer-term entrenchment of democracy. Like most new democracies, South Africa faces immense political and developmental challenges in a context of profound inequality, poverty, and social division. Any threat to ANC dominance, on this view, is also a threat to political stability and to the creation of legitimate political institutions. The ANC's widely shared self-conception as a national liberation movement helps it to contain conflict and to defuse racial or ethnic polarization, and its consensual mechanisms help it to socialize and control potentially anti-democratic leaders.

As Schire (2001) has recently emphasized, however, even on this positive account the ANC cannot absorb the many strains of transition on its own. Political competition is currently structured around historical (and therefore, he argues, ethnic or racial) affiliations, with no compelling ideological or policy conflicts setting the government against the opposition parties. For this reason, adversarial opposition – such as the (primarily White supported) Democratic Party's 1999 campaign on a 'fight back' manifesto – must inevitably be interpreted in polarizing racial or ethnic terms. Co-operative politics – as when the NP helped stave off economic crisis by its participation in the 1994–96 government of national unity, or in the IFP's current alliance with the ANC, which contains violence in KZN – is necessary to sustain democracy. Anti-ANC coalition-building, moreover, undermines the benefits of co-operation and courts a dangerous ANC counter-reaction.

By no means all commentators have greeted ANC dominance and the incorporation of the opposition as either necessary or positive developments. Critics on the right and radical left have each argued that the ANC is progressively closing down opposition and building the foundations of a new authoritarianism. 'Democracy', according to rightist critics Giliomee and Simkins, 'rests on countervailing power able to check tendencies towards authoritarian domination. The best counter is undoubtedly the presence of a strong opposition party that can guard against the erosion of the autonomy of democratic institutions and can replace a governing party that has outstayed its welcome.' Such sceptics argue that the ruling party is representing itself as the state rather than as a temporary incumbent, while other groups are losing the autonomy they require to compete. Ultimately the ANC's 'sheer preponderance of political power' will allow it to rule unilaterally and to abuse 'the advantages of incumbency and the state media to get re-elected time and again' (Giliomee and Simkins 1999: 337, 340). Because it is radically dependent upon the investment decisions of capital, they argue, the ANC cannot use economic populism to secure its rule and so must secure its mass base through concessions to organized labour and appeals to racial solidarity.

These cogent positive and negative reflections on ANC dominance are considered mutually exclusive by partisans and opponents of the government. Taken together, they pose a stark dilemma. While South Africa cannot afford robust opposition, or a fragmentation of the liberation movement, neither can it afford the consequences of deepening ANC domination. South Africa's democracy is not robust enough to cope with fluidity and party system reconstruction because of the need to build sound, legitimate, and trusted institutions. Yet the longer the ANC remains dominant, both electorally and in the executive, the more harm may be caused by state–party integration, patronage politics, opposition de-legitimation, and the abuse of incumbency. Such circumstances suggest only one attractive scenario. An extended period of ANC electoral dominance, over perhaps 10 or 15 years, will entrench the legitimacy of democratic institutions. At the same time, the government will face a real, but unrealized, threat of opposition defeat. It is latent opposition and non-electoral mechanisms, on this view, that will hold the government to account and check the abuse of concentrated power.

Holding a Dominant Party to Account

While there is an Anglo-American expectation that party opposition plays the central role in democratic accountability, the workings of non-electoral mechanisms are emphasized in contemporary international scholarship. Even within relatively stable multi-party systems, voting cannot be used in a graduated or targeted way to punish individuals or factions for their misdeeds. Electors face massive informational and collective action problems, and it is rarely clear to even the best informed voter who is responsible for which specific transgression. Even multiple parties vigorously contesting numerous elections across decades, as post-war Italy demonstrates, cannot prevent an entrenched collusion between the rulers at the expense of the ruled.

'Alternative government' is rare because there are so few genuine two-party or routine coalition-alternating systems. Western Europe primarily enjoys dominant-bloc coalition government, in which smaller opposition parties must act 'responsibly' to keep open the door to participation in future coalitions. New democracies, especially in presidential systems, have often lacked party system stability altogether, and have been subject to the vagaries of non-institutionalized leadership. Elsewhere, single parties have established themselves in positions of long-term dominance. In some cases, such as Mexico over an inordinately long period of stable one-party control, the party has proven a highly imperfect vehicle for holding political leaders to account (at least to the people). In others, notably post-independence India, the internal pluralism of the dominant party, and the influence of opposition 'parties of pressure' aligning themselves with governing party factions, helped secure extended if vulnerable periods of far wider accountability (Southall 2001; Reddy 2002). Reaction to Zimbabwe's 2002 election, crudely manipulated by Robert Mugabe's Zanu-PF to retain power, has undermined trust in the ANC's commitment to democratic transfers of power. The ANC leadership and a substantial body of opinion within the movement moved rapidly to applaud Zanu-PF's victory, and the South African parliament declared the election 'credible'. While there were clear diplomatic motives for the President's equivocation, the degree of genuine rather than merely tactical support for Zanu-PF among senior party figures and parliamentarians suggested that the ANC might not consent lightly to its own expulsion by the electorate.

South Africa possesses an array of constitutionally mandated checks to concentrated power, including legislative oversight, designated provincial powers, and independent oversight institutions: an auditor general, public protector, human rights and gender commissions, and an 'independent' reserve bank, broadcasting authority and electoral commission. The government is also constrained by a supreme constitution containing a bill of rights. The vulnerability of these checks to executive power became clear in the course of 2001, with the government's major arms procurement programme (see Chapter 8) the principal precipitant of crisis. The package is controversial for its scale, the naivety of its 'offset'-based financing, and for procedural irregularities including the incomplete briefing of cabinet. It was elements of high-level impropriety – discounted luxury cars for politicians and civil servants and insufficiently rigorous checks on involved parties' relations with subcontractors – that brought most widespread criticism.

A wide range of actors mobilized to raise and investigate these allegations, in what was in comparative terms an unusually public investigation of arms procurement corruption. The government's determination to control potential fallout from the investigations and to protect senior politicians and officials, however, led it to undermine the select committee on public accounts, the legislature's key and formerly nonpartisan oversight institution. It then took steps that, in the eyes of many, compromised the integrity of the offices of the auditor general and public protector. Already criticized for starving executive oversight bodies of resources, the ANC leadership seemed at times to be castigating opponents for investigating impropriety. Rather than building the legitimacy of democratic institutions, these actions served to reiterate the movement's commitment to party over state mechanisms of accountability.

The rapidity with which other formal checks to the executive were subdued during the arms scandal has thrown the role of the judiciary into relief. The constitution licenses an activist bench, and entrenches judicial independence unusually carefully through a Judicial Services Commission that insulates appointments from party manipulation. An activist bench, however, poses special problems in South Africa. The constitution sets out a number of socio-economic rights – to adequate health care, housing, education, water, and so on – which the executive is responsible for 'progressively' realizing. There have already been high-profile challenges to government legislation and action in areas such as housing policy and HIV/AIDS treatment, and trench warfare may set in between the judiciary, acting on behalf of specific complainants, and an executive committed to sectorally co-ordinated and incremental policy change. The judiciary is exceptionally vulnerable to a campaign of de-legitimization, especially because of its predominantly White composition, persistent racism in lower level court judgements, limited popular support for constitutional supremacy, and the lack of experience among the senior judiciary in making legal activism palatable to the political elite. Where the courts have found against the government, most recently over the treatment to HIV-positive pregnant women, ministers have equivocated in public as to whether court judgements must be obeyed, and already demonstrate a talent for quasi-compliance with judicial instructions. Just as the relationship between government and opposition parties cannot currently survive adversarial posturing, so judges and politicians alike will need carefully to moderate open conflict while they negotiate together and entrench boundaries between policy, politics, and the law.

Internal Pluralism

The opposition and the judiciary must clearly act with a degree of sensitivity in their negotiation with ANC power. The liberation movement, for its part, can entrench the legitimacy of democratic institutions only through willing compliance with judicial review and tolerance for adversarial opposition. Currently, however, the ANC represents a parallel political order, its external relations with the formal political system shaped by its need to accommodate its own internal conflict. An effective internal pluralism – an ability to encourage and respond to political and policy disagreement within its own organizational structures – is a prerequisite for accountability in a dominant party system.

Understanding the ANC is made difficult by the absence of systematic analysis of its political dynamics, membership, leadership recruitment, and generational change. The ANC's 'broad church' character combines histories and practices associated with exile, military organization, domestic struggle, trade unionism, communism, and imprisonment, which together help explain its complex behaviour. It displays both democratic and hierarchical aspects, and its style of conflict resolution is usually described as 'consensus building' This conventional and largely rosy assessment of the movement has been threatened by escalating conflict and centralization, traced by his critics to Thabo Mbeki's (Box 6.1) ascension to the presidency.

A product of exile, primarily surrounded by fellow exiles, Mbeki rose to unexpected prominence as Oliver Tambo's protégé and the son of

---

Box 6.1 Thabo Mbeki

Thabo Mbeki was born in Idutywa, Transkei, in June 1942, the child of ANC activists. Mbeki joined the ANC Youth League at 14, and quickly entered student politics. After his schooling at Lovedale was interrupted by a strike in 1959, he moved to Johannesburg, where he fell under the guidance of Walter Sisulu, and he was elected secretary of the African Students' Association. Mbeki's father Govan was arrested at Rivonia and sentenced to life imprisonment along with Nelson Mandela. Thabo left the country in 1962 for Britain where he completed a Masters degree in economics at Sussex University in 1966. Remaining active in student politics, he helped build the youth and student sections of the ANC in exile. After a period in military training in the USSR, he served in a variety of capacities in Zambia, Botswana, Swaziland, and Nigeria. During the 1980s he rose in the department of information and publicity, heading the ANC's Department of International Affairs from 1989, and thereafter became a key figure in negotiations with the NP. Mbeki became Deputy President of the new GNU. In December 1997, he became President of the ANC and in 1999 succeeded Mandela as state President.

---

a brilliant Robben Island-imprisoned ANC grandee. Hostile to the politics of the provinces – the level at which the movement primarily exists for its mass membership – Mbeki has allowed national institutions to impose their authority increasingly widely and aggressively. The exile ANC leadership adopted 'democratic centralism' from its SACP ally, which in the early 1990s famously abandoned such Stalinist techniques while retaining a long-range commitment to Marxism. The ANC leadership, by contrast, was obliged to embrace capitalism, but retained democratic centralism as an instrument of political management. Since 1999 the centre has tightened control over 'cadre deployment' at all levels of the state, and has further elaborated an ideology of primary accountability to the liberation movement. The National Working Committee appoints officers of the parliamentary caucus and parliamentary committee chairs, while insufficiently disciplined regional structures have been dissolved, and provincial premiers have been appointed against the wishes of provincial parties.

Centralization, of course, is hardly unique to South Africa, and should not be read as a reliable indicator of an increasingly imperial presidency. It is in part compensatory, a reaction to the emergence of refractory new fiefdoms in national and provincial government, but especially in the new integrated 'unicities' which enjoy a high and growing degree of autonomy. Centralization also reflects the growing professionalism of Mbeki's administration, and its determination to contain corruption and politicking in the provinces and municipalities. The idea of 'the struggle' once bound a diverse movement together, but new generations of career-minded activists are increasingly immune to traditional disciplines. Given the movement's poorly institutionalized systems of officer election and internal debate, a degree of enhanced control was perhaps inevitable. Such struggles are part of the stabilizing role that champions of ANC dominance consider its greatest strength, especially given the continuing presence in its ranks of independent-minded and forceful political entrepreneurs such as Winnie Mandela (see Box 6.2). It is indeed hard to see how conflicts of interest and opinion between trade union organizers and rural traditional leaders, for example, might be reconciled through any other conceivable set of institutions.

However, it is possible that the current leadership's limited political repertoire, and its enormous sensitivity to the personal and political

---

Box 6.2   Nomzamo Nobandla Winnifred 'Winnie' Madikizela-Mandela

Famous initially for her marriage to Nelson Mandela during his 26-year incarceration, political activist Winnie Madikizela-Mandela was born on 26 September 1936, child of a minister of the Forestry and Agriculture Department of the Transkei government. Educated at Shawbury school and University of the Witwatersrand, where she studied political science and international relations, Madikizela went on to work as a medical social worker at Baragwanath Hospital, conducting research into child mortality in Alexandra township that shocked her into political activism. Over three decades of political activism she was repeatedly detained, with a period of 18 months in solitary confinement in Pretoria Central prison and nine years of 'internal exile' in Brandfort where her house was twice bombed. Divorced from Nelson Mandela shortly after his release from prison, Madikizela-Mandela became an MP and member of the ANC's National Working Committee. Widely supported by activists, and possessing a popular touch that escapes the ageing and exile dominated leadership, Madikizela-Mandela's conflicts with senior figures in the movement and infringements of parliamentary protocol have been accompanied by frequent brushes with the law. Her conviction in April 2003 on multiple counts of fraud and theft has set back, but is unlikely to end, her maverick political career.

insecurities of the president, may suppress internal pluralism or even dangerously weaken the fabric of the tripartite alliance. The centre has sanctioned the abuse of internal and external opponents as 'unpatriotic' or 'ultra-leftist'.

Potential challengers to Mbeki's authority and position – such as Cyril Ramaphosa, Mathews Phosa and Tokyo Sexwale, brilliant and charismatic struggle leaders already 'redeployed' to the private sector – were investigated by the safety and security minister in 2001 for purportedly placing the life of the president in danger. Imposition of a conservative Growth, Employment and Reconstruction (GEAR) macro-economic strategy and an evolving privatization agenda have provoked many COSATU unions to act as external interest groups using public campaigns and strikes to re-establish influence. Over 2002 and 2003, the centre made more consistent efforts to stifle these leftist critics of emerging Africanist, Mbeki-loyalist, and pro-capitalist formations within the ANC.

The SACP, assigned key cabinet positions that put it into conflict with COSATU, has a membership that almost entirely overlaps with the ANC. Should opposition to the 'dual loyalties' of the communist leader-ship escalate, many might allow their SACP memberships to lapse. COSATU, by contrast, is a diverse and less manageable federation of unions, brought into alliance with the ANC primarily through anti-apartheid struggle. Many union leaders are hostile to the ANC's self-conception as heroic vehicle of national liberation and resent the preponderant voice of exile elites. COSATU has opposed government positions on a range of sensitive issues, and many of its leaders resent the growing roles of personal loyalty and racial solidarity in internal Alliance debate. The left's weakness, however, was highlighted by its January 2002 agreement that contentious issues henceforth be confined to party structures, within which there is growing unwillingness to cross senior party figures or members of major power blocs.

If the tripartite alliance is increasingly strained, there are also some doubts about the oft-presumed robustness of the ANC's voter base. Three important cautions are in order for those who view the move-ment's dominance as inevitable. First, a growing number of voters express themselves dissatisfied with the performance of the government, and indicate that they might be available to an appropriate opposition party. The ANC is therefore not insulated against effective challenge should its performance deteriorate. It may be the current absence of credible opposition parties reflecting the interests of the discontented, rather than unshakeable affiliation, that secures current ANC control. Popular participation seems to be in precipitous decline while ANC membership, after a period of centrally driven region and branch 'reconstitution', has reportedly fallen from 300 000 in 1999 to less than 90 000 today. Second, the implications for ANC support of slow economic growth, increasing unemployment, AIDS, and changing patterns of income and wealth distribution, are little understood. Comparativists have identified relationships between higher income levels, low inequality, and democratic persistence, but the implications of these findings for South Africa – with its complex and racialized reference groups – are uncertain.

Lastly, while analysts have explored the potential for urban populist opposition, we do not know very much about the too-easily assumed control of the ANC over the political allegiance of the rural poor. The social forces that can destroy or sustain democracy often lie in the countryside, a fact overlooked by most contemporary democratization scholars (Yashar 1997). While the Black middle class and organized labour each has a strong voice in the movement, the far larger constituencies of the rural unemployed, the informally employed, the old, and – increasingly – AIDS-victims, have little leverage. Macro-economic conservatism precludes large-scale rural patronage, public service delivery has run aground beyond the towns, rural job-creation is a lost cause, and the political fallout of the AIDS pandemic remains difficult to predict. The unusual political sophistication of South Africa's rural areas at the same time militates strongly against the effectiveness of consolatory populist racial appeals. As the centre is merely forced to shore up its support beyond the cities, this will in itself further strain the ANC's labour and urban alliances.

External and Economic Limits to Poor Government

Many sceptics of the durability of checks and balances and internal pluralism nonetheless believe that wider, and often international, political and economic forces will help contain ANC power. The government is vulnerable to the exit of capital and skills, depends on business confidence to encourage investment, and is sensitive to pressure exerted by the countries of the OECD zone. The government has carefully avoided economic populism, and demonstrated vulnerability to external political pressure, for example, in its April 2002 policy reversal on anti-retrovirals, when the AIDS issue threatened to discredit the New Partnership for Africa's Development with its G8 partners.

External influences, however, do not provide a reliable inoculation against bad government. In the area of corruption, for example, international indices suggest that South Africa is both major source and recipient of improper payments. The ANC faces powerful incentives to deal with allegations within party structures, especially since corrupt behaviour is hard to bring to court, and so many cadres are implicated in questionable if not illegal activities. Unwillingness to permit high-profile prosecutions, and allegations of obstruction to investigation at the highest level, suggest that party leaders harbour the illusion that the problem can be politically managed. If corruption becomes entrenched, and passes certain thresholds of normality, only then will an external constraint come into play, as South Africa becomes regarded as 'just another African country', its international credibility seriously damaged.

Potential capital flight has also preoccupied and constrained the government; but this sword is double-edged. The exaggerated conservatism of macro-economic policy, itself a reaction to the fears of external actors, may have entrenched structural obstacles to faster growth and deepened investors' concerns that sustained inequality must bring an eventual political counter-reaction. Because 'perceptions' are elusive, and subject to game theoretic complication, their management always leaves government vulnerable to vicious circles of collapsing credibility and confidence. The potential emigration of skilled workers provides a similarly unreliable limit to government freedom of action. More than 200 000 South Africans left permanently for English-speaking countries alone between 1989 and 1997, and analysts predict the next five years might see anywhere between 30 000 and 200 000 further departures. Émigrés, usually beneficiaries of South Africa's highly unequal educational provision, often bewail the limitations of the new South Africa in order to ease the guilt of exile. Rampant xenophobia has meanwhile limited legal in-migration to a few thousand per year with the economic benefits of immigration disregarded (Crush and McDonald 2003).

The greatest danger these external constraints pose is that while they are advertised as non-negotiable, they are easily reinterpreted as 'western' impositions. Conservative macro-economic policy is viewed by many South African intellectuals and activists as merely a redefined form of African subjugation to structural adjustment. While a growing number of skilled Black workers are now joining White émigrés overseas, emigration is still sometimes welcomed as creating space for Black advancement (while excessive sensitivity to the interests and fears of potential emigrants justly generates resentment). The failure of international business to invest heavily in post-apartheid South Africa is widely attributed to racism and Afro-pessimism. For 'economic reality' to serve as a check on government actions it will need to be interpreted in a less politically charged way.

Conclusions

South Africa's fundamental political dilemma is that liberation movement domination is a necessary condition for the entrenchment of democratic practices and institutions, but it is also and at the same time a threat to them. Electoral defeat at the best of times represents a poorly calibrated and ineffective reaction to governing party misbehaviour, and in contemporary South African conditions it would represent a cure worse than almost any conceivable disease. Many other mechanisms – formal checks and balances, internal pluralism within the ANC, and the external impositions of capital – continue to constrain the actions of the executive, but each has fundamental drawbacks. The centre is progressively colonizing independent checks on executive power, in the legislature, provinces, and independent oversight offices. The ANC's assorted alliances are becoming increasingly conflict-ridden and cannot be relied upon to absorb societal antagonisms. Capital and skills flight set dangerously unpredictable limits to action. In each case, there is a threat of counter reaction should political entrepreneurs abuse racial polarization to defend poor governance, cadre corruption, or perverse policy.

This complex but precarious structure of accountability now faces a series of blunt political challenges, each following its particular logic, but causally interconnected in complex ways. AIDS will reduce growth, damage business confidence and investment, and accelerate skills flight. One may speculate that it might destabilize the tripartite alliance, foster opposition in the countryside, and hamper the battle against corruption and financial mismanagement. Corruption, if it should escalate, will reduce the state's capacity to manage AIDS, and provide a rationale for destabilizing opposition alliances. Skills and capital flight themselves may precipitate a reaction against business. Such potential relations between complex processes help explain the variety and uncertainty of prognoses for the country's future.

President Mbeki's capacity to pilot his country through these rough waters has been much debated. Critics argue that his limited ability to generate trust and affection leaves the centre dangerously dependent on organizational manipulation and the rhetorics of race and national liberation. A more balanced appraisal would register the impossible combination of qualities the office of president currently demands, and the problems any leader would have faced in succeeding a living legend like Mandela. A state with so little autonomy from capital, that cannot control crime, extract service payments, or monitor its borders, is unlikely to pose any immediate threat to the opposition supporters and ANC critics who control the country's wealth. (Indeed, it may be that they pose far too slight an immediate threat.) Restrictions on ANC internal debate, however, will lead to bad policy, a fear given credence by the debacle over HIV/AIDS. Natural science represents a formally open structure of knowledge, in which conventions of contestability and evidence are founded on the willingness of powerful scientists to accept correction. The most successful political leaders may likewise be those with the least compliant followers, whose inevitable errors are therefore subject to correction (Grint 2000). The growing tendency among ANC supporters to identify the person of the president with the cause of national liberation itself might prove problematic under even the most sure-footed national leader.

It is an inescapable conclusion, unwelcome to those who fear protracted one-party dominance, that a cohesive tripartite alliance, enjoying sustained and co-operative relations with opposition parties, offers South Africa the best hope of entrenching its highly imperfect democracy. The movement's popular reach and legitimacy help to render the majority's dire circumstances politically supportable, and its institutions ameliorate and contain the society's diverse conflicts. However, if the advertised benefits of a collaborative political order, marked by consensus and compromise within and between parties and institutions, are to be realized, this will require a more open and democratic-spirited politics that the ANC is currently able to muster.

7

Culture, Ideas, and Issues

This chapter introduces South Africans' popular and high cultures, and explores their intellectual preoccupations and everyday debates. The first section investigates the country's music, theatre, dance, film, and art, before going on to explore everyday social interaction in urban, suburban, and peri-urban contexts. The second section examines the key elements of national intellectual life. The final part of the chapter investigates highly charged issues that are the currency of everyday argument and debate, among them unemployment, crime, corruption, and HIV/AIDS.

Professional Cultural Production

The seemingly innocent word 'culture' is dangerously slippery. Academic social scientists sometimes talk of cultures to refer to the 'maps of meaning' through which people make sense of their world. A practice that is quite accepted in one culture may not 'make sense' in another. Interacting with different ways of living may produce confusion and disorientation, and we sometimes even say that a traveller experiences 'culture shock' upon entering unfamiliar fields of experience that do not correspond to her cultural expectations. More everyday use of the term is also contested. In its western European lands of origin, the concept of 'high' culture refers to the artistic, expressive, and aesthetic practices and performances of a society: its poetry, literature, painting, and sculpture. 'Low' culture, by contrast, refers to the ways in which people live their daily lives – their sports and pastimes, their practices of sociability and friendship, their popular music, recreational drugs, and styles of dress. This distinction between high and low culture, and the identification of the former with a set of professional artistic practices, is the product of particular (western) historical circumstances, and it carries with it an assumption that the artist, poet, or composer stands at some distance from everyday society. It therefore does not help us to understand societies like South Africa in which oral traditions, dance, religious practice, music, and other cultural artefacts are deeply woven into, and sustain, ordinary social life.

South African intellectuals are today wrestling to reconcile their conflicting conceptions of the cultural. The 'intercultural dialogue' that a post-apartheid nation so requires is inhibited by distinct historical experiences and understandings of the realm of culture. In particular, 'culture' was used in the apartheid period as a vehicle for promoting racial and ethnic identities, to justify a discriminatory allocation of resources to Europeans, and as an ideological weapon in the propagation of the naturalness of culturally distinct 'communities'. Like other colonial populations, European settlers in Southern Africa used their economic and political power to enforce their conception of cultural value. Typically, 'high' cultural practice was understood as an attainment of Whites, which gave expression to the cultural superiority of European civilization. European forms – such as classical music, ballet, opera, theatre, and fine art – were used to reiterate and reinforce White settlers' relationship to the colonial heartlands, and to celebrate the higher civilization they supposedly exemplified. State funded provincial arts councils were used to channel monies towards these cultural productions for the benefit of primarily White audiences. The Afrikaner nationalist project reinforced these tendencies while successfully achieving for Afrikaans a status of formal parity with English in education, the media, and the arts.

The aesthetic traditions and practices of Africans were treated by official cultural professionals as the products of static tribal cultures, significant primarily for their role in perpetuating tribal distinctiveness and division. Even many highly educated Africans, who were usually the children and grandchildren of mission-school educated elites, embraced a European conception of cultural hierarchy that denigrated African history and culture. Ironically, however, apartheid destroyed the cultural infrastructure that had allowed an African elite to aspire to proficiency in the ways of western cultural practice. As cinemas, theatres, galleries and museums were segregated fully from the 1950s, and the centres of urban African culture were bulldozed and their communities dispersed, African intellectuals were forced to consider with fresh eyes the virtues of cultural products rooted in Africa. Such necessarily inconclusive investigations were sometimes couched in terms of a search for 'authenticity' or the 'traditional'. Under later apartheid such debates became even more sharp and double-edged, because the state moved to build new ethnocentric cultural practices for 're-tribalized' Africans in order to reinforce the system of Bantustans. The notion that there must exist a fundamental division between (superior) European and (inferior)

African culture was supplanted by the high apartheid agenda of 'separate development', which was premised on the fundamentally conflictual relations between cultures and ethnic groups. Anti-apartheid politics also influenced cultural production. 'The struggle' worked its way into almost all sites of public expression – church services, sports events, funerals, and almost any form of community meeting – as well as the political rallies that became an opportunity for new forms of dance, music, and poetry. It also helped neutralize the effects of retribalization, and to oppose the new class of African cultural practitioners and traditionalists employed to advance the agenda of ethnic distinctiveness. Professional cultural practitioners, most of them White, developed their own ways of subverting the assumptions of the apartheid order, and many of their organized artists or performers collectives ultimately became ANC-aligned networks of non-governmental organizations.

The end of 'the struggle' had a variety of repercussions for cultural professionals and practitioners. For primarily White and historically advantaged professionals, non-racial democracy has brought upheaval and soul-searching. Foreign funding has largely evaporated. Domestic anti-apartheid artistic coalitions failed to inherit control of the resources and cultural infrastructure of the state (which the ANC's department of arts and culture seized in asserting its 'vanguard role'). After an extensive process of consultation with artists, educators, and administrators in 1994, a new National Arts Council has been created whose function is progressively to redirect resources away from the traditionally Eurocentric arts councils towards historically unrecognized and undervalued forms of creativity in music, dance, crafts, and community performance. The resultant funding slack for high culture is to be taken up by private sponsorship – a problematic response, given that business and the power of markets are each predisposed to support a limited range of high cultural outputs.

Largely insulated from these developments, English- and Afrikaans-language writing have continued on their respective pre-1994 trajectories. Those writing primarily in Afrikaans, and especially a new generation of women authors, demonstrate openness to international influences and an ability to embrace a rapidly changing social reality. English-language writing, by contrast, inhabits an increasingly barren human and socio-political territory. While the fine arts and English literature have certainly not flourished since 1994, it is in the traditional theatre that resources and self-confidence have been most undermined by the end of the struggle. The 'protest theatre' of the 1980s was primarily a self-celebratory preoccupation of Gauteng's urban middle-class Whites (Fleishman 2001). Apartheid or broader colonial themes continue to predominate in today's theatre, although more introspectively and uncertainly, and it has not managed to broaden its audiences beyond its traditional middle-class base. While Black and women performers are now commonplace, moreover, directors continue to be almost always male and disproportionately White, although a new generation of formally trained Black graduates is emerging.

The transformation in dance and opera has been strikingly more successful. While western 'theatre' has stagnated, African theatrical dance has achieved economic viability. South African dance has been one of the country's few major cultural exports, with local companies performing to acclaim in the United States and Europe. As in many other areas of cultural production, South Africa's strength has developed from the abandonment of conservative conceptions of the traditional (be it European or African) and through moves towards fusions of style and choreography. In opera, classically trained Black performers have been equally successful internationally, and belatedly among domestic audiences, since 1994.

Music has been undergoing a period of more general and rapid innovation and development. The apartheid period saw a progressive racial segregation of musical output as the cosmopolitan communities that sustained non-racialism were destroyed and their populations relocated. Towards the end of the apartheid era, an international cultural boycott in protest at apartheid isolated musical artists and audiences from international interaction. At the same time, however, music was an instrument of resistance and opposition to apartheid, and the onset of democracy created a vacuum or a loss of purpose among the country's artistic and cultural communities as well as presenting to them new opportunities.

Choral music, which has played an especially important role in South Africa across the past century, has been least affected by these changes. South African choral music achieved international prominence after the participation of isicathamiya performers Ladysmith Black Mambazo in Paul Simon's 1986 *Graceland* album. Church, school, and adult choirs remain the major popular musical activity in the country. This music is often based around an early twentieth-century fusion between four-part choral singing – which originated in Victorian British hymnal – and American minstrelsy, which was acquired from late nineteenth-century vaudeville tours, and provided greater opportunity for social critique. 'Traditional' influences came later and been less significant, as have the effects of other primarily American innovations such as rock 'n' roll and country music (Impey 2001; Erlmann 1999).

While the search for resilient authenticity in such historically complex forms has continued, younger South Africans have been drawn to more intricate fusions between a range of domestic and international musical traditions. As elsewhere, popular music production has diversified and internationalised, and products such as techno-raves and house music have been introduced and reworked in urban culture. Local historical and continental influences have been important. The township jazz seemingly displaced by the forced removals of the 1950s and 1960s has been rediscovered and is being reconfigured, partly under the influence of historically more developed and innovative West African jazz and blues traditions.

The Culture of Everyday Life: Urbanization and Suburbanization

The progressive urbanization and suburbanization of the South African population has wrought massive changes in the nature of everyday community life. For most Africans, of course, migrant labour has been a familiar part of the life cycle for almost a century. In the early decades of the twentieth century, legislative changes to undermine African rural societies and destroy Black farming economies made it increasingly difficult for rural Africans to survive without remittances from the core urban economy. A pattern of migrant labour was enforced through which young men and later women would pass much of their lives in and around the 'white' cities of South Africa.

Migrant labour created both generational and gender divisions. Young men and later women worked away from their families, in hostels, backyard shacks, or informal settlements close to places of work, as part of a cosmopolitan and sometimes vibrant urban and peri-urban culture. The old, disproportionate numbers of women, and young children remained in the Bantustans, heavily dependent on remittances from the towns and later upon systems of state support like the government pension. The annual cycle of migrancy would end each December as millions travelled to the Bantustans to spend the Christmas season with relatives and children. Such a pattern of cyclical migrancy is common to developing countries as urbanization involves stalls and reversals for individuals, even as the aggregate urban population is growing. Yet South Africa was locked by apartheid into an extremely extended process of displaced and cyclical migration.

Everyday life for most South Africans is still marked by a duality of experiences and relationships, with communities, families, and individual life cycles straddling the chasm of existence between desperately impoverished rural areas and relatively affluent urban centres. Rural areas often still fall under the partial sway of traditional modes of authority, through which hereditary male leaders have the power to allocate land and other economic resources. Much of the rural population is old, although there are many young children undergoing their schooling away from the crime of the townships, in the care of grandparents or other relatives. Rural areas are dependent on savings, urban remittances from the more affluent and younger population living in the towns or peri-urban settlements, and the state pension system – supplemented by a desperate survivalist mode of agriculture. Many of the former homelands are not 'rural' at all, but rather immense and densely populated townships located at great distance from economic opportunities. Unemployment, poor health care, limited public services, high levels of child mortality, and HIV/AIDS plague these areas. Everyday life is a battle against poverty and disease, punctuated by spells of mostly fruitless pursuit of pitifully remunerated labour. Women's plight is especially severe, as they undertake backbreaking chores of water collection, firewood gathering, and agricultural work.

The cities, towns, peri-urban townships and urban informal settlements contain a diversity of opportunity and experience, but rarely the crushing hopelessness of most rural life. Cities remain sharply segregated, with the White suburbs preserved today by income inequality rather than legally enforced division. There are some long-established townships, formerly native locations, which provide relatively good public services and access to urban labour markets. But these are few in number. Most urban Black people live at considerable distances from economic opportunity in townships designed to separate them from White suburbs and city centres. The search for income dominates daily life for most township residents. What work there is, is largely poorly paid, and often physically draining. Workers must be up long before the sun to take crowded and expensive mini-bus taxis, buses, or trains tens of kilometres to places of work (or hoped-for work). A domestic worker, for example, may deliver her own children to a township crèche before undertaking an arduous journey at the end of which she prepares for school the children of a suburban household.

Townships and informal settlements, however, are not merely places of hardship. Everyday social interaction is marked by courtesy, and opportunities for hospitality are embraced. Both church and popular music and sport – primarily soccer, a rare sport enjoyed by South Africans of all races – thrive on a young population. 'Shebeens' or taverns are numerous and alcohol and drug intake can be considerable. Township communities, however, are marked by exceptionally close systems of moral scrutiny. They are often genuine communities, with shared political histories (often of informal settlement and organization to demand services) as well as clear institutions for regulating crime and deviance. Far from undergoing moral breakdown, as some outside analysts suggested in the early 1990s, townships continue to represent extremely dense networks of moral relationships in which mutual obligations are strong. Indeed, such relationships are necessary for survival in difficult and uncertain economic circumstances. It is partly because of such expectations of mutual respect and obligation that the scourge of crime is experienced as so intolerable and inexplicable a social evil.

Public service provision has made a substantial difference to the lives of many established township residents, although urbanization brings more informal and unserviced households each year. Despite very uneven provision of tarred roads and drainage, civil engineering standards are often relatively high in formal townships. Households with mobile 'cell' phones, electricity for lighting and leisure, and external running water and sanitation are now commonplace in urban areas. Car ownership – an especially significant economic resource given the location of the townships, but also an important signifier of status – is growing, as are small businesses devoted to auto maintenance. Church halls, sports facilities, and community halls accommodate community, musical and religious activities and there has been a flourishing of non-political voluntary associations.

With the crucial difference of vastly greater economic opportunity, the suburban life of White South Africans (and especially Afrikaners) shares many features with that of urban Africans. Despite the potential alienation that comes with suburbia, Whites often maintain traditions of hospitality and politeness towards outsiders (although not necessarily towards Black South Africans). Traditional South African gender roles and an orientation towards a unique outdoor lifestyle remain in place. The high value automobile is also for White men the most significant object of status, although the ideal of both a BMW and a four-wheel drive vehicle is now beyond most families. International, and especially American cultural influences are evident everywhere in White as in Black South Africa, notably in the music, movies, shopping malls, and American suburban lifestyles that Whites have in recent decades embraced. Despite these parallels, however, the social lives of Black and White South Africans still rarely cross and their residential patterns remain largely segregated. Interaction between races is usually also interaction across classes in the workplace, with Whites typically of higher status. Africans rarely visit Whites' homes, except as workers, and few Whites ever visit an African suburb or township.

Broadcasting

One area in which social infrastructure is primarily shared is in the realm of public broadcasting. Although many wealthier South Africans use subscription services, the South African Broadcasting Corporation (SABC) is a very significant provider of television and radio programming to all South Africans. A staunch supporter of apartheid oppression in the 1980s, SABC relaunched itself as a public service broadcaster immediately before the ANC's accession to power in 1994, so averting what might have been a fundamental overhaul at the hands of the new government. Under the regulatory control of an Independent Broadcasting Authority (IBA), the SABC is formally committed to independence from government and private sector interests, to the promotion of diversity, and to the pursuit of the public interest.

The most visible result of the SABC's new mission was a reconfiguration of television channels in 1996, through which formerly English and Afrikaans channels were allocated primarily to Nguni and Sotho languages, with only one channel devoted to domestic English-language programming (although cheap American and British imports fill the schedules of all three channels). In radio, a medium especially important for many rural South Africans, commercialization and regional licences have increased choice and diversity, including in local languages. The SABC, however, has many critics, who highlight its unfair competitive advantage (through public licence fee revenues) and the continuing predominance of English. As with broadcasters elsewhere, the SABC has come under pressure from changing technologies and the internationalization of the media, which has brought new channels – both cable and free to air – and a diversity of outside voices and influences.

SABC executives have been under heavy and persistent pressure from the ANC over news and current affairs reporting, and the broadcaster's new found editorial independence is already compromised (Teer-Tomaselli 2001). It has been unwilling to affront senior ministers by aggressively reporting high level corruption, maladministration, or external policy failure, be it in Zimbabwe or the New Partnership for Africa's Development. However, public interest broadcaster principles are widely understood within the SABC, and they have been defended on occasion, including episodic exposés concerning government mishandling of the HIV/AIDS epidemic. In addition, while local content has been quite low at around 37 per cent of all programming, the SABC has achieved around 50 per cent local content during evening prime time, mostly through its commitment to news and current affairs reporting. Furthermore, the government's hostility towards editorial independence – both in the SABC and commercial broadcasters – has been accompanied by the readiness of ministers and officials (but not the president) to appear on air and present the government's case.

Ideas

South Africa's history has been shaped by the overarching intellectual systems associated with White Supremacy, Social Darwinism, segregation, and apartheid. Apartheid's opponents, for their part, often embraced abstract and totalizing intellectual traditions such as Marxism and Black Consciousness. Professional academic scholarship has been racialized and prone to formalism and functionalism. Given these historical weaknesses and oppositions, perhaps the most astonishing feature of the country's current intellectual life is the high degree of conformity and consensus it embodies.

The collapse of apartheid ideology and the 'triumph of democracy' were elements in the wider international intellectual reconfiguration of the past two decades. The collapse of the Soviet economy and the end of the Cold War signalled the end of the only viable alternative to capitalism and undermined socialist and social democratic doctrines. A 'Washington consensus' set out in greater detail new expectations of trade liberalization, market deregulation, and fiscal conservatism. At the same time, the project of universal liberal market capitalism advanced through a wave of democratization and market opening between the mid-1970s and the turn of the millennium.

South Africa's professional political class capitulated in the face of these international ideological forces. A broad national consensus emerged in the early 1990s negotiations for macro-economic stability, fiscal prudence, liberalization of trade, the rule of law, and representative democracy. Socialism and the public ownership of the means of production are no longer credible alternatives to market capitalism even for avowed leftists. Recent conflict between the ANC-aligned trade union movement and the government over privatization has, in fact, been couched in mostly non-ideological and pragmatic terms.

Africanism and Modernism

Behind this seeming consensus, however, there lie disagreements that are in some ways more fundamental. These concern the historical struggle between Africa and the West, and the relationships between African systems of ideas and those – including socialism, liberalism, and communism themselves – that originated in Europe. The notion of a distinctive African universe of ideas and values has been founded both historically and philosophically in opposition to colonialism (just as western intellectuals have historically used their characterization of Africa to define their own 'civilization').

One important influence on social commentary has been the fusion of Black consciousness with an Africanist field of scholarship, creating a distinctive Africanist style of intellectual discourse and political commentary. While positive and emancipatory in intention, Africanist scholarship has been confronted with the inescapable catastrophe of the failure of post-colonial Africa. In global terms, states that were comparable in the 1960s – say Ghana and South Korea – are now separated by a developmental gulf. In absolute terms, African per capita incomes have stagnated or fallen for two decades, and political instability, collapsing state capacity, and rapacious political elites are widespread. Western (and to their enemies 'Eurocentric' African) scholars have located Africa's crisis in the failure of the state to fully penetrate civil society, so remaining hostage to it. Africanist scholars, by contrast, argue that the continent's communities have failed to hold the African state to account, and have therefore fallen prey to it. For one eminent scholar, Mahmood Mamdani, Africa's distinctiveness lies in mechanisms of 'indirect rule' by means of which colonial powers enforced their authority at arm's length. Land remained communal or 'customary', and tribal leadership was selectively imposed or reconstructed at the behest of the colonial powers. Indirect rule 'at once both reinforced ethnically bound institutions of control and led to their explosion from within. Ethnicity (tribalism) thus came to be simultaneously the form of colonial control ... and the form of revolt against it'. Free and fair elections cannot remove the 'decentralised despotism' that marks all postcolonial African politics (Mamdani 1996: 24, 289, 286).

White South Africans advance a 'first-and-third world' conception of their society, used routinely to explain their country's predicament to foreigners. The 'first world' contains highways and hospitals, affluent consumers and suburbs, advanced technologies, and a sophisticated financial system. It has enjoyed political rights, issue-based voting, and western political institutions, and its inhabitants (who happen to be White) are rational thinkers. The third world is characterized by townships, poverty, subsistence agriculture, migrant labour, and devastatingly low productivity. Its social life is marked by patronage, clientelism, tribalism, and violence, and its intellectual world circumscribed by superstition, and primitive ethnic division. This vision encompasses both a Victorian conception of civilization and post-war notions of development, White South Africa forever a European entity superimposed upon a borderless African continent.

Yet South Africa is not marked by such oppositions and neither is its politics a typical product of colonial rule. Nineteenth-century wars of dispossession, mass population displacement, and enforced changes in social organization undermined the communal land control Mamdani identifies as crucial to indirect rule. The mineral revolutions transformed social structure in late nineteenth- and early twentieth-century South Africa. Proletarianized and urbanized South Africans, moreover, with their sophisticated urban intellectual and political cultures, have been capable of remarkably detached understandings of exploitative social institutions. South Africa's rebellion against apartheid was not in any way confined to a war against institutions equivalent to 'indirect rule', even if these institutions did indeed bear the brunt of direct protest. Opposition to apartheid was also often self-consciously anti-ethnic, political, urban, unionized, and ideological.

Issues

Some of the central issues and debates in South African politics and society emerge directly out of its history of colonialism, segregation, and apartheid. Others, while they may have quite distinct origins, are profoundly shaped by these fundamental divergencies of perspective, and by the racialisation that can easily enter almost any disagreement. Yet, the two issues most widely and consistently debated across society, unemployment and crime, concern all South Africans (see Table 7.1). Work is a practical problem for the majority of South Africans whose employment does not meet their needs or ambitions or is simply unavailable. Debate over jobs takes many forms: educated Whites tend to complain that affirmative action is making their employment prospects impossible, notwithstanding the evidence that Whites have benefited handsomely over the past decade from changes in the structure of the job market. For most South Africans, jobs are simply scarce, and their pursuit is a constant preoccupation.

Table 7.1   The changing public agenda 2002

Important issue facing the country	% raising the issue as important*
Unemployment	84
Crime	35
Poverty	28
HIV/AIDS	26
Housing	22
Education	15

* Up to three issues (unprompted) per respondent.

Source: Data from Idasa 2002a.

Crime, and especially violent crime, impacts on almost everyone in the society, although it is undeniably at its most relentless for poor urban communities, for women, and for children. Crime statistics are notoriously unreliable, and in South Africa the government has intermittently imposed moratoriums while attempting to revise data collection and crime classification practices. It seems clear that violent crimes such as murder, attempted murder, rape, and assault are at very high levels indeed. Reported property crime, however, is relatively modest given the extreme levels of inequality in the society. There are strikingly higher rates of crime in the wealthier provinces such as Gauteng and Western Cape.

Attitudes towards crime have been shaped by a history in which the police were the instruments of popular oppression, and politically motivated violence was widespread. Other societies in transition have suffered growing levels of crime, especially where constitutional changes have, like South Africa's, obliged the police to abandon conviction through forced confession for evidence-based prosecutions. Today, communities are broadly committed to a variety of anti-crime initiatives, and the moral opprobrium heaped upon criminals has intensified. The 120 000 strong South African Police Service (SAPS), moreover, may be moving towards greater effectiveness in its criminal policing practices. Levels of training have improved. New approaches, such as 'sector' policing, which bring police officers into closer contact with communities, are being piloted. SAPS has been working with other departments in a National Crime Prevention Strategy to disrupt the cycle of violence within communities, and to remove some the conditions (such as poor street lighting) that allow criminals to flourish.

The success of these strategies is likely to be tightly circumscribed. Wider social conditions, such as growing unemployment and persisting inequality, are not conducive to their success. Crime is disproportionally committed by young men and youths, and South Africa, already a young society, will see a growth in this age cohort across the next decade. A substantial proportion of young people, moreover, will grow up without one or both parents as a result of HIV/AIDS. These orphaned children – suffering from social rejection, shame, loss of education, and limited economic opportunity – will be more likely to engage in (and to fall victim to) criminal activity than their non-orphaned peers (Fourie and Schonteich 2001).

The criminal justice system presents a range of further obstacles to the war on crime. Relations between criminal and national intelligence agencies have been poor. The prosecution service has not worked harmoniously with the detective branch, although reforms to this system have been put in place to ensure that evidence that can support prosecution will be more reliably collected in future (Steinberg 2001). The prison population of more than 170 000, kept in accommodation designed for less than 100 000, includes more than 57 000 unsentenced prisoners who are awaiting trial or sentencing. Almost 30 000 unsentenced juveniles were held in custody in 2001. Recidivism rates are unknown but can be assumed to be high. The prevalence of rape and gang organization within hostel-type accommodation, moreover, is likely to have led to exceptionally high rates of HIV and AIDS among the prison population.

While violent crime is a preoccupation of most South Africans, corruption is a less widely debated issue. Corruption impacts especially hard on the poor, as acquiring the necessary permits, papers, and authorizations for everyday survival can become a painful and costly process. However, according to a 2002 survey (Idasa 2002a), just one in 20 South Africans was victim that year to corrupt officials demanding bribes to obtain government services. High level corruption has until recently been less widely debated, although the country has a very long history of official and politician enrichment. Public disenchantment has been growing in provinces with entrenched corruption such as Eastern Cape. Trust in political leaders has been everywhere declining, and opposition parties are experimenting with anti-corruption rhetoric. At the same time, the proportion of people who think 'most or all officials' are involved in corruption fell from 50 per cent in 2000 to 27 per cent in 2002 (Idasa 2002a).

The direct instruments through which the government is attempting to create a Black middle class and to reduce racial inequality in the distribution of wealth – affirmative action and Black economic empowerment – are not matters of great public debate at present. Indeed, other than the complaints of Whites about displacement from work, these policies have proven relatively uncontroversial, presumably because it is widely accepted that the injustices they are designed to ameliorate are indefensible. Racialized argument flares more quickly around seemingly tangential issues that expose fundamentally different assumptions about social change. Many Black South Africans, for example, intuitively suspect that Whites' criticisms of political leaders in neighbouring African states are racially motivated (and some critics of Mugabe have certainly demonstrated that their sympathies lie with Zimbabwe's White farmers only). White South Africans, moreover, can react with astounding incredulity to employment equity policy, or even to racial quotas in nationally representative sports teams, despite the history of systematic segregation and the apartheid-era destruction of Black sporting traditions. In everyday interaction across races, however, South Africans drift towards issues that are relatively uncontroversial within the society.

Certain other political debates, prominent elsewhere, are widely disregarded in South Africa. Despite a flurry of interest while Johannesburg was hosting the 2002 'Rio-plus-10' World Summit on Sustainable Development, for example, environmental issues have a low political profile. Signatory to a number of key international conventions – including the 'Montreal' convention on ozone, 'Basel' on cross-border waste, 'Stockholm' on Persistent Organic Pollutants, and 'Kyoto' on global warming – South Africa nonetheless has an exceptionally poor environmental record. It is a major greenhouse gas emitter, and the world's sixth largest producer of carbon dioxide. South Durban, the Vaal Triangle, and the North of Cape Town suffer extreme problems with organic compounds, sulphur dioxide, and particularite pollution. The country combines urban problems characteristic of any emerging economy – vehicle and ground water pollution, hazardous industrial and medical wastes, illegal landfills, and noise pollution – with rural soil degradation, overgrazing, poor quality and limited availability of water, and agricultural pollutants. Both inshore waterways and offshore marine habitats are also heavily degraded.

Many of South Africa's most substantial environmental impacts can be traced to the historical strength of primary extractive activities, minerals processing, and associated heavy industries. This sector is a major polluter in its own right through the dumping of solid wastes from gold ore separation, liquid waste pits, radon gas and silicon dust releases, and acid and chemical disposals. In addition, these energy intensive activities are supported by an electricity generation sector that relies predominantly on coal and that does not scrub emissions for sulphur. Household energy consumption continues to be dominated by polluting sources such as coal, wood, and paraffin.

The constitution states that everyone has a right to an environment that is not harmful to their health or well-being and to have the environment protected for future generations. Government policy is likewise attractively premised on three key ideas: that people should live in harmony with nature; that clean water, air, and land should be made available; and that green spaces should be a part of every citizen's immediate environment. Using the concept of 'sustainable development' (development which meets the needs of the present without comprising the ability of future generations to meet their own needs) the government has elaborated a legislative framework for managing the impacts of public sector pollution. The government is also moving cautiously towards an integrated pollution and waste management strategy – aimed at prevention rather than treatment – for the private sector. Whether these initiatives will be able to overcome the entrenched opposition of South Africa's many established polluters – including the state itself – is an open question.

One issue that cannot be evaded is HIV/AIDS. Given the relatively early stage in the HIV/AIDS epidemic, and limited experience of such a severe health crisis, its scale is much clearer than its implications. Southern Africa's poverty, war-driven population movements, and hostel-based migrant labour system, have provided ideal conditions for the spread of the human immunodeficiency virus. South Africa has the world's largest absolute number of HIV-positive people, perhaps 5 million out of its 45 million population, and can expect 7 million AIDS-related deaths, and 2 million AIDS-orphans, by the end of the decade. Spread by sexual contact, AIDS impacts most heavily on the working age population, raising dependency ratios, reducing productivity and generating knock-on effects (such as the loss of a family home) when a breadwinner dies. Moreover, as a quarter of skilled workers and perhaps one in seven highly skilled workers become infected by 2005, AIDS will also severely undermine the human capital in the public service, business, and the professions that will be required to address the pandemic's consequences.

On paper, South Africa's democratic and unitary state possesses the perfect attributes for fighting HIV/AIDS. Divisions within the ANC, however, have led to a fiasco of policy inconsistency and intellectual confusion, and the movement has been unable to progress to a pragmatic policy consensus. The institutions set up to spearhead the battle against the disease are virtually inoperative, while stigma and confusion continue to undermine efforts at prevention. Some attribute this to President Mbeki's 'dissident' or 'denialist' position on the natural science of the disease. In accordance with this, he claims that the causal relationship between HIV and AIDS is merely a 'thesis', that antiretroviral treatments are more toxic than HIV itself, and that his senior AIDS advisory panel rightly contains a balance of orthodox and dissident voices. A second and related explanation highlights the long-standing role of race and sexuality in African nationalist discourse over HIV/AIDS elsewhere on the continent. Attributing AIDS to western degeneracy, and especially to homosexuality, some conservative nationalists as early as the 1980s castigated theories of the African origins of HIV as racist scapegoating. In March of 2002, an unofficial and unattributed paper entitled 'Castro Hlongwane, Caravans, Cats, Geese, Foot and Mouth and Statistics: HIV/AIDS and the struggle for the humanisation of the African', was circulated to the ANC's National Executive by Mbeki-confidant and election strategist the late Peter Mokaba (Mokaba *et al.* 2002). This discussion document interpreted HIV/AIDS as a creation of the continent's enemies, described findings that the virus originated in Africa as 'insulting', and echoed the president's late 2001 claim that conventional AIDS science views Africans as 'promiscuous carriers of germs ... doomed to a mortal end because of an unconquerable devotion to the sin of lust' (Forrest and Streck 2001).

The government is in addition unable to treat anything like the projected numbers of infected citizens, given intractable shortages of health professionals, infrastructure, and rural services such as water. AIDS-related expenditure demands across the public service as a whole, moreover, will severely limit the feasible growth of health and welfare budgets. Other governments in the region may have used the rural–urban divide to help manage AIDS health and governance impacts, and to limit the crowding out of urban public expenditure. While the ANC has been bolstering once-shaky alliances with traditional leaders, however, it cannot expect that its own poor, unskilled, and stigmatized AIDS sufferers will continue to lie down and die quietly in the former homelands. An unusually sophisticated rural population, with extended historical experiences and networks in urban areas, will migrate or return to the towns and cities in search of treatment and hope, and stigmatization is unlikely for long to inhibit the political organization of those affected by HIV/AIDS.

Since the government cannot finance the delivery infrastructure necessary for universal access to medical treatment, it will presumably build treatment partnerships with business, perhaps through a restructured health insurance system. This dispersal of responsibility for ameliorating the suffering to come, however, is as much a political as a technical imperative. One may speculate that politics could take an unhealthy turn, as citizens – confronted by a political and administrative infrastructure itself eroded by AIDS – can muster less concern for 'democracy', find selective treatment unjust, refuse to pay for public services, or follow political leaders promising relief from despair. A key party political concern for ANC strategists may be that it must not become identified with a total war against the disease that it will inevitably lose. Here the historical significance of the liberation movement in the eyes of some of its leaders may play a role. The ANC's 1994 triumph represented for them the culmination of a century of anti-colonial struggle on the continent, and signalled the start of an African renaissance. On this interpretation, a proud national liberation movement that takes history to be on its side has collided too violently with the intolerable reality of an AIDS catastrophe, and it is the truth that has had to give way.

8

South Africa and the World

Modern South Africa bears the imprint of a history of domination by external forces. The South African state was created at the turn of the twentieth century by the world's then greatest empire. Its peoples are a product of continental migratory drift, cross-oceanic slavery, and colonial aggression. Its more recent history was profoundly influenced by the Cold War, and today it is vulnerable to the dynamic of a new period of economic globalization. While the most powerful tradition in the study of international relations interprets the self-interested state as the central actor of international politics, South Africa's twentieth-century governments mostly failed to define, let alone pursue, a national interest. The state has been a key actor in its region, building and undermining institutions to promote the immediate goals of its governments. Pretoria used military and economic muscle to prevail over weaker neighbours, while also making use of a conventional variety of co-operative instruments, including multilateral institutions, treaties, and diplomatic agreements. Even in its immediate neighbourhood, however, military, business, and parastatal relationships, rather than intergovernmental ones, have dominated interstate conflict and co-operation.

Beyond the immediate Southern African region, the state has enjoyed only limited ability to impose itself in the face of powerful international economic and political forces. International strategy in the apartheid era was driven by a relatively small elite within the ruling National Party, serving the perceived interests of a minority of the country's people. NP strategic goals were contested by a parallel international ANC diplomatic and military system, which managed increasingly to isolate Pretoria in the international community and to secure a right to be heard as the legitimate voice of the South African people in international forums. Today the ANC can claim to represent the people of South Africa, and it has fashioned a realistic strategy of multilateral international, continental, and regional diplomacy. However, it has not embarked upon any genuine exercise to build national consensus around what would seem to be appropriate and realistic foreign policy goals.

Modern South African International Relations

In the first half of the twentieth century, South Africa's international relations were framed by its position in the British Empire. Notwithstanding domestic division, she participated in the Great War and was rewarded in 1919 with the former German possession of South West Africa, today Namibia, which became her protectorate. South Africa's domestic economy was thereafter closely but perversely tied to the fortunes of the international economy. From the abandonment of the Gold Standard to turmoil in the contemporary Middle East, tumult in international affairs has often raised demand for the 'safe haven' of gold, boosting South Africa's foreign exchange earnings and raising domestic demand. The global industrial wars have also benefited South Africa, as a marginal participant in fighting, yet one with the ability to export into the war economy of its allies. The period of international despair, commencing with the great depression of the 1930s and culminating in the devastation of the Second World War, was for these reasons an era of great prosperity for South Africa. Her primary commodity, gold, appreciated dramatically in value in the 1930s.

As the Second World War approached, the economies of the industrial powers turned to re-armament leaving open markets for primary and manufactured outputs. From 1940, there was a major expansion in the defence industry as, with British assistance, major investments were made in the manufacture of military hardware for the Allies' war effort. South Africa ended the war a manufacturing economy for the first time, with a rapidly urbanizing population – the latter's predominantly Black composition being one of the precipitants of the electoral triumph of the NP under the apartheid slogan in 1948. Thereafter South African foreign policy moved rapidly into line with the racial priorities of the NP, and the relationship to British imperial interests was severed. These developments occurred in the context of two great structural changes in the international system, and in how it was understood. The first was the emergence of the Cold War, a four decades long struggle in which the Soviet Union and its satellites and proxies faced off against an alliance of capitalist powers, led by the United States but supported by all of the world's major market economies. The second development was the idea and the reality of the 'Third World', as European powers ceded their colonies, and Asia, Africa, and Latin America entered an era of partial political autonomy but continued economic dependency.

South African external policy was trapped between the contradictory logics of these twin processes. In the 1950s, White South Africa was committed to racial supremacy and segregation in a continental context increasingly marked by African nationalist assertion and colonial withdrawal. The claims of inherent White supremacy and the need to civilize the native were becoming internationally unacceptable as justifications for White domination. At the same time, the Cold War allowed the South African government to elaborate a rhetoric of pro-Western anti-communism, and a conception of natural alliance with the United States and Europe. This rhetoric found echoes in the West in an age of uneasy decolonization and the nascent era of Cold War by proxy. While the 1960s deepening of the Cold War in this way strengthened Pretoria's hand in Washington, the decade also saw the emergence of civil rights movements in the United States, and a constituency opposed to the racialization of the state under apartheid. South African foreign policy was increasingly a matter of playing off the country's fairly limited strategic significance against its growing unpopularity.

The creation of the Bantustans in the 1960s, and the elaboration of the doctrine of 'separate development', tried to align racial domination with the growing movement of post-colonial independence. The homelands, the government indicated, were to be independent African states – as viable and natural as Lesotho, Swaziland, or Botswana – that would permit African 'nationals' to fulfil themselves through their own systems of government. In part because of intense diplomatic lobbying and public campaigning by the exile ANC and an international anti-apartheid movement, none of them was ever to secure international recognition.

Pretoria's position was nonetheless buttressed until the mid-1970s by a number of strategic advantages. The first was the existence of a substantial White dominated power bloc in the region, which shared common interests in the maintenance of the status quo. For Pretoria, the collapse of authoritarianism in Portugal, and the hasty consequent withdrawal of that power from Angola and Mozambique in 1975, had very significant repercussions. Former 'buffer states' were replaced by the self-characterized 'Front Line States', with an avowedly common agenda of displacing the apartheid regime. South Africa, however, could still rely on the fraternal support of Rhodesia, which had pursued its own policy of White domination after unilaterally withdrawing from British control in 1965. South Africa, moreover, had extended its control over South West Africa (Namibia), which had become a virtual province and in which apartheid had been instituted from 1964.

Pretoria had further significant foreign policy resources at its disposal. South Africa remained the predominant economy in the region. Even front line states vociferously opposed to the apartheid regime had to accommodate themselves to the reality of their dependence on its transport infrastructure, technical skills, the remittances foreign workers sent home from its mining economy, its key exports, and its role as a market for their products. Smaller and landlocked states, in particular, suffered an extreme dependence. The 'liberated' states to the north thus found it impossible to exert a continuous and unequivocal pressure on the apartheid regime.

At the same time the military capacity of South Africa was unrivalled. The national defence force had only 20 000 members at the start of the 1960s, but this had grown to 80 000 by the end of the 1970s. The defence industry built upon wartime production was bolstered in the 1950s through the nurturing of domestic research and development capability. In 1963, the United Nations introduced a voluntary ban on arms sales to Pretoria. While this was to become mandatory only in 1977, important states, including the United States in 1964, introduced voluntary prohibition early on. Pretoria's response was to redouble domestic capacity–building, creating Armscor (Armaments Development and Production Corporation, later Armaments Corporation of South Africa) in 1968. Armscor rationalized and consolidated private and public sector capacity, developed domestic self-reliance in pivotal technologies, and built the foundations upon which a major export industry arose in the 1980s (Smaldone 1997: 350–4).

The 1978 ascension of former Defence Minister P W Botha to the prime ministership signalled an escalation in the role of the military in politics. Externally, South Africa became more exposed after Rhodesia reached independence as Zimbabwe in 1980. Botha's multifaceted strategy involved alliances or accommodation with smaller and weaker foes, covert aid to rebels in neighbouring states to destabilize their unfriendly regimes, and the creation of increasingly fearsome deterrence and counter threat capabilities – including sometimes the use of pre-emptive strikes in episodes of open aggression. The regime attacked the forward bases of the ANC in the front line states, abducting and assassinating ANC cadres and destroying military assets. Major attacks took place in Mozambique (1980, 1981, 1983, 1987), Lesotho (1982, 1985), Botswana (1985, 1986, 1988), Zambia (1986, 1987), and Zimbabwe (1982, 1986) (see Smaldone 1997: 339–46).

Domestically, under the rubric of 'total strategy', the regime committed itself to a counter-insurgency approach. Botha reconfigured the executive to create a 'state within a state' dominated by military and intelligence interests. A National Security Management System brought some order to the security and intelligence apparatus. One cabinet committee – the State Security Council (SSC) – secured ascendancy over other parts of the state, implementing 'total strategy' with the support of its own extensive secretariat and administrative capacity. The SSC brought together ministers of defence, foreign affairs, justice and law and order with senior military, police, and intelligence chiefs. At the same time, the military–industrial complex developed in scale and intensity, with the workforce of Armscor, for example, growing from 10 000 in 1974 to around 33 000 a decade later. Despite the UN ban on arms exports, South Africa exported to more than 50 countries in the 1980s, including African states Zaire, Gabon, Morocco and Malawi, and insatiable consumers Iran and Iraq. The 1980s also saw the culmination of South Africa's nuclear, chemical and biological weapons programmes, with at least six nuclear warheads built out of domestically enriched uranium by the mid-1980s. These weapons were dismantled in 1991 under pressure from the United States, and Pretoria signed the Nuclear Non-Proliferation Treaty.

The ascendancy of the military establishment, however, was always partial. Despite progressive militarization, 1989 South Africa was in just 44th place in the world in terms of military spending as a proportion of GNP and just 49th in terms of the size of its forces (Smaldone 1997). The security establishment was domestically politically vulnerable to a White electorate dissatisfied with NP strategy, and internationally after the 1989 unravelling of the Soviet empire undermined Africa's Cold War dynamic and undercut the power of anti-Communist rhetoric. A falling away of Soviet arms shipments into the region fundamentally changed the balance of forces and the incentives facing actors. The United States pressured regional powers to accept Namibian independence in 1990, together with a joint South African, Soviet, and Cuban withdrawal from the conflict in Angola. In the early 1990s, as the region faced climate-induced drought and famine, South Africa even mobilized its technical and financial resources to assist its neighbours, signalling a fresh conception of relations between former adversaries.

The year 1989 also transformed the relationship between the South African state and its foreign sponsors. In the 1980s, United States policy was driven by a desire to ameliorate Soviet influence in the region and to entrench the NP regime as a bulwark against communist ideology and practice. The significance of South Africa, otherwise a small state in an area of very limited strategic importance to the United States, was enhanced by the country's minerals wealth, and particularly the abundance of platinum, gold, and uranium. In compensation for the reduced strategic salience of the Cape sea routes, South Africa had emerged as a producer of many of the scarce metals vital to the technologies and industries of the future, and remained geographically within striking distance of the major resource reserves of Angola and Congo.

While the United States enforced the UN voluntary arms embargo, and refused to recognize independent homelands, successive administrations continued a policy of 'constructive engagement' with Pretoria. This stance was justified for the United States executive by the purported need to maintain influence over an otherwise obdurate regime and by the costs that sanctions would bring to the poor in South Africa. However, congressional opinion is also important in the making of United States foreign policy and anti-apartheid politics played a special role in congressional–presidential branch conflict in the 1980s. Reagan's hawkish White House was widely criticized by leaders in the federal legislature. The fractious congressional black caucus, in particular, found in apartheid an issue around which it could sustain its internal coherence. One consequence was the passing over a presidential veto in 1986 of the *Comprehensive Anti-Apartheid Act*, which laid down a complex system of disincentives and sanctions to United States' investment in South Africa, prohibited loans, and curtailed existing economic contacts. Two-thirds of firms in the United States active in the Republic sold all or part of their holdings (Byrnes 1997).

South Africa's relations with its more significant trading partner, the European Union, were still more complex. By 1992, the EU accounted for more than half of all foreign direct investment in South Africa, and was the market for more than 40 per cent of South African exports, as well as the source of a variety of loans, grants, and aid monies. Of the two key trading partners within the EU, German companies continued their operations in South Africa with little disruption. The United Kingdom meanwhile shadowed Ronald Reagan's policy of constructive engagement under Margaret Thatcher, and through the mechanism of the Commonwealth, in which the United Kingdom was a major force, fought off efforts to construct a more aggressive programme of sanctions against Pretoria.

By 1989, a variety of domestic actors were converging upon a negotiated settlement (see Chapter 1), and the collapse of the USSR added fresh momentum to this process. The ANC's allies in the South African Communist Party were undergoing a far-reaching overhaul of their orthodox Cold War pro-Moscow stance. Moderates within the Afrikaner establishment and business were promising a negotiated settlement, and their opponents no longer had the external justification of anti-Communist defiance to fall back on. Apartheid's fundamental mechanisms of population control had turned out to be unsustainable, and the political foundations of NP dominance were crumbling. After 1989, regime change in South Africa was almost inescapable.

Foreign and Defence Policy under Mandela

The early 1990s brought an unwinding of the relationships between the security state and the establishment, and a new focus on the practical problems that would come with any political settlement between the NP and the ANC. For the next decade, the longer-term strategic priorities of the new South Africa jostled for attention with the more immediate imperatives of remaking the military and creating a stable and coherent state. Within the ANC, idealist and pragmatic schools of thought battled for supremacy.

Practical imperatives were legion. First, the transition to democratic rule had to be managed in a context of immense suspicion on both sides, but especially ANC concern about the willingness and capacity of the military to protect an ANC government threatened with ethnic conflict or even civil war. The military and intelligence establishments had to be discreetly brought on side and into the negotiated settlement. At the same time, the armed forces had to be unwound from the state, a process well advanced under de Klerk. While the defence force had no real escape from this change, its co-operation was bought at considerable cost. A swathe of promotions, early retirements, sunset clauses, and other incentives were offered by the incoming government. More painfully for many, the ANC effectively abandoned any systematic attempt to identify and punish those in the military and intelligence responsible for apartheid era atrocities.

Second, the various military and intelligence structures of the ANC and the government had to be integrated as quickly and effectively as possible. On the military front, this involved the incorporation of not just the ANC's armed wing, Umkhonto we Sizwe (mK), into the defence force, but also the PAC's military arm the Azanian People's Liberation Army (AZAPO). Both mK and AZAPO forces were unevenly trained in traditions quite different to those prevailing in the South African Defence Force (SADF). In addition, the homelands' military forces had to be absorbed. The merger process was accomplished but at great human cost to many of the younger generation of mK volunteers who did not find a permanent place in the defence force and represent a potential source of political difficulty for the government in the future.

A third set of problems concerned the industrial complex attached to the military, especially the Denel offshoot of Armscor. As domestic and international military spending fell across the late 1980s and into the 1990s, Denel shed labour alarmingly, and with it skills, foreign exchange, and technological and other comparative advantage. In 1994, weapons exports were still over a billion Rand and employment in the sector over 50 000. One of the incoming ANC government's earliest decisions was to maintain manufacturing capacity in this sector and to continue to promote military exports – even though many ANC supporters believed this ran counter to the disarmament agenda advanced prior to 1994. Proponents of an industrial adjustment strategy to reconfigure South Africa's weapons-building capacity for less malign uses were vetoed by the pragmatists who saw this sector as essential for jobs and exports.

The uncertain relationship between the pragmatic and moral dimensions of foreign policy was evident in a watershed article on the ANC's likely post-apartheid foreign policy agenda that appeared in 1993 under the name of Nelson Mandela (1993) in *Foreign Affairs*. This article set out broad principles to guide South Africa's post-1994 external relations, including the promotion of human rights and democracy, the encouragement of peace through negotiation and arms control agreements, the integration of African concerns into foreign policy, further cooperation through the Southern African Development Community, and integration into global trading relationships. In practice, almost all of the benign intentions behind this agenda were under attack from the moment the ANC came to power in 1994.

As Mandela's presidency got under way, with the uninspiring figure of Alfred Nzo at the helm in Department of Foreign Affairs (DFA), the ANC's lofty moral ambition repeatedly ran aground on the rocks of realpolitik. The honeymoon between Mandela and Clinton's New Democrats did not survive the first few month's of ANC rule. Mandela harangued the United States for failing to deliver on what he believed were promises of massive aid and investment. The United States for its part bewailed the ANC's refusal to abandon ties with what it characterized as rogue states or terrorist regimes – in Cuba, Iran, Libya, and Syria. Mandela developed a doctrine of universality through which the Republic suspended judgement on the behaviour of other states, a position which sat uneasily with the commitment to high morality with which it had commenced its rule. Its attempts to lobby against the United States' trade boycott of key ANC ally Cuba played especially badly in the United States, as did its later support for the Palestinian cause and for Zanu-PF in Zimbabwe.

Mandela's universality hit the hard wall of reality in the form of the People's Republic of China, when South Africa tried to finesse the conflict between the authoritarian behemoth and the newly democratic Republic of China (Taiwan) with which South Africa had very significant trade and investment relations. After a poorly managed attempt to satisfy Beijing that South Africa was an exception to the usual rules of diplomatic recognition, Pretoria was forced to sever full diplomatic relations with Taiwan in full glare of international publicity. Closer to home, Mandela then tried to intervene in a human rights crisis in Nigeria, in order to prevent the arbitrary execution of human rights activists including poet Ken Saro-Wiwa in 1995. Mandela severed diplomatic relations, only to be condemned by other African leaders for high-handedness and interference, and by domestic liberation movement critics for acting on behalf of the West against a fellow African regime. Inflated rhetoric about the common interests of Africa's peoples was exposed by the violence and xenophobia that marked (and continues to mark) treatment of immigrants in a region beset by population displacements. There are several million illegal immigrants in South Africa, popularly viewed as competitors for work as well as made scapegoats for disease and crime. The ANC in government has maintained much of the internal policing apparatus of apartheid and uses it aggressively to curtail the opportunities of migrants to South Africa or even to expel them.

Alongside the moralizing aspect of South Africa's foreign policy under Mandela, there was a tendency to embark upon grandiose projects and to overstretch the nation's limited resources. Peace in Africa is in the interest of South Africa, but the ANC's ongoing preoccupation with conflicts elsewhere, including Ireland and the Middle East, is neither realistic nor endearing to potential allies. South Africa's leaders exaggerate the uniqueness of the society's transition to democracy, and overestimate the lessons it can teach other societies (whose problems are often far more intractable than those Mandela and de Klerk surmounted in 1993 and 1994). Many domestic commentators mirror apartheid's claim that South Africa contains first and third worlds, or the developed and the undeveloped world, and so claim that its leaders have some special place as interlocutor between North and South (Barber and Vickers 2001: 343–4). Yet, as we saw in Chapters 3 and 4, South Africa is a fairly wealthy developing country with an appalling record of violence and inequality. Far from indicating any special capacity to ameliorate inequalities and consequent social conflicts, this reality may demonstrate that the society is quite exceptionally poor at coping with such challenges.

Rethinking Foreign Policy for the Twenty-first Century

South African diplomacy and external strategy during the four decades after 1948 were driven by the desire to defend and advance the domestic agenda of White domination. The ANC's honourable initial instincts from 1994 were to shake the very foundations of realpolitik and to advance an international agenda worthy of a 'New' South Africa. However, under Thabo Mbeki's tutelage, external strategy has embraced a more pragmatic and limited conception of international politics.

Critics claim the government still lacks any clear sense of priorities in foreign affairs and that there has been too little debate about the nature or content of national strategic interest. Certainly, little effort has been made to forge a national consensus through debate, and government has pursued many contradictory objectives – including the mollification of domestic constituencies – simultaneously and sometimes uncertainly. As Mbeki has rightly recognized, however, the central external problem facing all African states is their progressive marginalization in the international economy. Economic development elsewhere has lifted hundreds of millions out of the despair of poverty in the past two decades, and may continue to improve the lots of still more numerous millions in China, India and Latin America in coming decades. Africa has been largely excluded from these momentous developments (see Table 8.1). The key question for African leaders is how to participate in this economic order, to attract investment, to trade, and to become part of the value adding supply chains that make up the international economy. Africa has suffered severely from falling commodity prices, decreased investor interest, spiralling debt burdens, and policy prescriptions that have hindered rather than promoted economic development.

The Mbeki government has registered this priority and its actions suggest that it has embraced the fundamental role of foreign policy in

Table 8.1   Global annual per capita income growth, 1975–99

Region	% world population	% growth per capita income
East Asia and the Pacific	31	6
South Asia	23	2.3
OECD	19	2
Latin America and the Caribbean	8	0.7
Arab states	4	0.3
Sub-Saharan Africa	10	−1

Source: Adapted from UNDP 2002.

advancing business interests. Early ANC cabinets allowed moral ambition and the pragmatics of doing business to come into conflict, creating unproductive stand-offs and embarrassment for South African and foreign representatives. Conflict with the EU and the United States in trade negotiations rapidly disabused them of the notion that leverage is best exerted from the moral high ground. Today, the central role of diplomatic representation overseas is unashamedly to secure export markets, business partners, and foreign direct investment for South Africa.

If the primacy of economic affairs is now widely appreciated, however, the content of the national interest in this area is still poorly defined. One difficulty is that South Africa's currently important economic relationships are not aligned with liberation movement theology. Western Europe and the United States remain South Africa's key trading partners and sources of investment, skills and technology, while important constituencies within the ANC consider that its destiny lies within Africa. The liberation movement, such Africanists claim, can catalyse continental renaissance, and bring the continent into a new relationship of equality with the West. The density of diplomatic, trading and other ties with western Europe and the United States is for them a cause for concern rather than for celebration. Both international financial institutions such as the World Bank and International Monetary Fund (which demand that prudent fiscal and monetary policy and liberalized markets are preconditions for loan finance) and trans-national corporations are viewed with huge suspicion by many ANC intellectuals. Some intellectuals, moreover, seek not merely a pro-African agenda, but an anti-Western one, and the Department of Foreign Affairs has come under some pressure from the ANC parliamentary caucus to build its diplomatic infrastructure around such ideological rather than economic imperatives.

In addition, a lack of realism still bedevils government ambitions. Among the 'new' foreign policy issues that the ANC has championed since 1994 are sustainable development and anti-pollution initiatives, population control, mechanisms for dealing with communicable diseases, arms proliferation, migration issues, democratization, and human rights concerns. Yet South Africa itself has a record that is questionable at best with regard to almost all of these issues: it is a major polluter, one of the world's leading greenhouse gas emitters, a substantial arms exporter, and an intolerant host to migrants which is losing key skills through out-migration. It has, moreover, questionable status in the field of public health. There has consequently been little international tolerance for South Africa's claims to speak with authority in these areas.

One major external policy scandal concerns the highly controversial 1999 Strategic Defence Procurement Package (widely known as 'the arms deal'). The government had conducted a national defence review in 1995 with a view to determining the future role and structure of the military. Its findings were endorsed by parliament in 1998, and government moved very rapidly into a procurement phase, with cabinet announcing as early as September 1999 that technical analysis, affordability studies, tendering, and selection processes were complete. The package was to amount in total to more than R20 billion over eight years (or R30 billion over 12 years if an option to procure additional equipment was exercised). The package included 'industrial offsets', or counter-trade agreements, in terms of which the suppliers undertook to carry out procurement or other economic activities within South Africa to a value of more than R100 billion.

Controversy surrounded the deal almost from the moment it was signed, bringing allegations of corruption in the procurement process from an opposition member of parliament, and demands from the legislature's public accounts oversight committee for clarification of unexplained irregularities in procurement and potential conflicts of interest. The package has become controversial for its scale, the naivety of its 'offset'-based financing, for procedural irregularities including the incomplete briefing of cabinet, and for a seemingly endless escalation of costs. High-level impropriety – including discounted luxury cars for politicians and civil servants and insufficiently rigorous checks on involved parties' relations with subcontractors – brought heavy criticism. Many actors have raised these allegations, in what has been a comparatively open and public investigation of arms procurement corruption. The government's determination to contain fallout from the scandal and to protect senior politicians, however, led it to undermine parliament's select committee on public accounts. In the course of 2003, the allegations surrounding the arms deal reached as high as the office of the Deputy President. Not for the first time in international affairs, a major arms procurement exercise has precipitated a domestic political crisis.

The African Union and NEPAD

Altogether more promisingly, 2002 was a significant year in the diplomatic history of the continent, seeing the launch of two significant and related initiatives – the African Union (AU) and the New Partnership for Africa's Development (NEPAD). The African Union is successor to the ill-starred Organisation of African Unity, a divided and latterly inertial body, which failed in the context of postcolonial economic and political crisis to identify or prosecute continent-wide goals and interests. The AU proposes an immensely ambitious framework for co-operation between states, ultimately moving towards a quasi-federal relationship on the model of the European Union. Its institutional innovations include an African parliament, the evolution of a common African judicial system, and closer economic relationships to be secured by means of customs unions and free trade agreements. The AU project has potentially wide emotional appeal, because it promises to end decades of subjugation of Africans to foreign economic, cultural, and political domination. It proclaims that Africans, through their own collective efforts, will achieve a cultural and intellectual equality with their peers in the West.

While South Africa has come late to the AU process, the philosophical underpinnings of its ambitious agenda were spelled out by Thabo Mbeki in a speech to the US Corporate Council on Africa in 1997, when he astonished his audience with the claim that 'the African Renaissance is upon us!'. The notion of continental renaissance flies in the face of conventional Western assumptions about the stagnation of Africa's economies and the failure of its political leaders to develop sustainable pathways to prosperity. Dismissing such 'Afro-pessimism', proponents of African renaissance claim that a new kind of inter-state relationship can be built out of the unhappy heritage of conflict in Africa. Sceptics counter with the claim that the architecture of the AU cannot function in today's Africa, and serves only to place still more power in the hands of a cross-national clique of venal and corrupt leaders.

The second major initiative of 2002, the New Partnership for Africa's Development (NEPAD) is sometimes described by its proponents as the AU's economic blueprint. It will be integrated into the AU machinery, once this is fully operational, probably in 2004 or 2005. NEPAD is the most significant effort to assemble a strategic approach to Africa's overall developmental challenges. It is scarcely a programme for concrete advance, so diverse and diffuse are its goals, and so ambiguously worded its proposals for action. But it does assemble a series of priorities for the continent that may provide the basis of concerted action by governments, donors, and private investors. Among the central pillars of NEPAD have been the notion that it should act to co-ordinate the economic relations between African states collectively and the developed world. Thus it would seek a common continental position in multilateral trade negotiations, a common strategy with regard to development aid, a single debt reduction policy, as well as dealing on a collective basis with the promotion of foreign investment in Africa, conflict resolution, and infrastructural investment. More problematically, but essentially, NEPAD is also informed by respect for an open society and for democracy. While peer review mechanisms for corporate and economic governance and for financial systems can be made credible, it is not yet clear whether issues of political governance can ever be satisfactorily addressed.

NEPAD's ambitions were dealt a severe blow in 2002 by the G8 partners' refusal to pledge any support for new infrastructure or debt relief. They offered, moreover, only the possibility of further negotiations over trade and aid issues. Western critics of NEPAD highlight weaknesses in voluntary 'peer review' governance mechanisms. They point in addition to the failure of African states to rationalize their own chaotic systems of regional economic communities (of which there are some 14) before demanding access to developed country markets. NEPAD's ability to flourish within the AU is also open to question. Organisation of African Unity (OAU) bureaucrats are strongly critical of South African hegemony, Anglo-French tensions seem ineliminable, and conflicts of interest and opinion surround key players Nigeria and Libya. It seems likely that NEPAD will integrate into the AU in a relatively modest form as an agency through which international and regional trade negotiations will be conducted and as a mechanism for co-ordination of cross-country infrastructural and other investment projects.

Some of the more ambitious continental programmes conceived for NEPAD may eventually be implemented at regional level, perhaps through a re-energized Southern African Development Community. SADC contains a more coherent and potentially manageable group of states than the AU, and it would be less riven by the rivalries that threaten any continental body. Good governance mechanisms and trade liberalization might in future be advanced hand in hand in South Africa's more immediate neighbourhood. At the same time, however, South Africa's immediate neighbours include Zimbabwe. This country's recent dismaying descent into economic and political crisis has provided an object lesson in the limits of South African power even in the heart of the SADC region.

Mechanisms for Foreign Policy Making

The creation of a coherent post-1994 foreign policy making process has thrown up considerable institutional challenges. The incoming Mandela government brought together quite distinct and formerly bitterly opposed traditions in diplomacy and intelligence, while transforming the content of external policy. At the same time, officials of the Department of Foreign Affairs were inevitably regarded with distrust and hostility, and the Defence Ministry was unavoidably preoccupied with structural reviews, procurement policy, and the creation of an integrated defence force. The Department of Trade and Industry and the Treasury have secured ascendancy in foreign trade, investment, and economic relationships. Even more markedly, the Presidency has dominated the cluster of International Relations Peace and Security (IRPS), intervening sometimes heavy-handedly in foreign investment promotion, the AU's creation, the Zimbabwe crisis, and NEPAD, among others. The Presidency has also worked hand-in-glove with external actors such as the Government Communications and Information Service (GCIS), the African Renaissance Institute, and the parastatal Eskom.

Much to the chagrin of some parliamentarians, movement discipline has largely restricted ANC caucus members to ritual affirmations of executive-driven policy. Members of the foreign affairs oversight committee have often been briefed on policy change but none of them can claim an active role in shaping it. The public accounts select committee, as we have seen, was even disabled as a result of its nascent investigations of the arms procurement process. While there is a parliamentary committee dealing with Africa-related foreign policy issues, it is almost inoperative and defers to the Foreign Affairs committee on issues of potential sensitivity to the Presidency such as NEPAD and human rights in Africa.

Opposition parliamentarians have been more vocal than ANC colleagues on foreign policy, especially with regard to the crisis in Zimbabwe and the conflicts in Palestine and Iraq. However, the primarily White and English-speaking leadership of the official opposition Democratic Alliance does not enjoy popular legitimacy when commenting on the behaviour of liberation movements such as Zanu-PF, a lack of authority shared by think tank the South African Institute for International Affairs. Indeed, DA attempts to steer a course closer to the United States and Israel on middle east conflicts were exploited by the ANC to portray it as sympathetic to imperialism and a 'new apartheid' in Palestine. ANC leaders have used these more distant international crises quite skilfully to promote the ANC as a leader within the international non-aligned movement, to build upon existing relationships and sympathies in the Arab world, and to defuse domestic tensions over more local policy with regard to Zimbabwe.

The influence of the Presidency in foreign policy making has been controversial. While the current President has unmistakably offered leadership and moved decisively across a complex diplomatic terrain – most impressively in a series of breathtaking peace initiatives in central Africa – his office has alienated many skilled officials and wider stakeholder constituencies in the state and business. Only over coming years and indeed decades will the success or failure of Mbeki's consistent and determined external strategy become evident.

9

South Africa in the Twenty-first Century

The struggle against apartheid threw South Africa into an unhappy international prominence. The country continues to carry a weight of expectation for those who hope for a more prosperous and less conflict-ridden future for the world's developing countries. South Africa is now at the heart of an emerging project to remake Africa's political life and transform its economic prospects. She is also at the centre of the struggle of the countries of the South, for a more equitable international trading order. Yet the practical potential of such initiatives is hard to assess: the complexity and depth of Africa's multiple crises almost defy comprehension let alone remedy. South Africa's economic weight, moreover, makes her inadvertently a regional bully, and her political ambitions have stirred rivalries with other African powers.

Pretoria also has problems of her own closer to home. The country's triumphant 1994 election signalled the start of a new era of uncertainty for all South Africans. The increasingly desperate and violent struggle of the National Party establishment to maintain minority political domination was thankfully over. The task of creating a less divided and unequal society still lay ahead. This chapter offers a preliminary assessment of the liberation movement's achievements in addressing this legacy after a decade of African National Congress rule. It goes on more tentatively to predict what the future will hold for a society that, more than almost any other, has divided and surprised scholars and political analysts.

The Economy, Human Development, and Welfare

Economic advance is a prerequisite for the political stability and social reconciliation to which South Africans aspire. It is through the creation and more or less fair distribution of wealth that the many conflicts of the nascent democracy will be ameliorated or exacerbated. The record of the ANC on this score deserves credit. In the early post-war period, a golden era for the economies of many nations, South Africa grew at between 4 and 6 per cent per year for two full decades. In the years that followed, however, falling commodity prices, political conflict, and structural rigidities in the economy all played a part in a lamentable legacy of low and erratic growth. The NP, moreover, tossed aside fiscal responsibility in its desperate efforts to cling to power.

When the ANC swept into office in 1994, it inherited a dangerous budget deficit and an escalating national debt. The movement's achievement in abandoning socialism and presiding over a decade of deficit reduction is considerable. ANC leaders have inculcated an awareness that good public services require not more but better public spending. Yet the liberation movement has had to draw heavily on its reserves of popular trust, as it has presided over a stagnation of formal sector employment. Perhaps 40 per cent of those who desire work are denied it. Inequality has deepened and too little progress has been made in de-racializing inequalities of ownership and income.

Government has made most progress in making available basic public services – water, sanitation, electricity, decent schooling, housing, and healthcare – that were previously the exclusive privilege of Whites. The obstacles overcome and the improvements in quality of life that have often resulted cannot be overemphasized. A wide swathe of Black South African society today lives in households with basic services and amenities unthinkable 10 years ago. Yet the very poor are still denied the dignity of access to 'universal' public services by user charges and economic insecurity. Like other developing countries, South Africa has to run simply to stand still, as the demands thrown up by urbanization, rural decay, and social dislocation accumulate day in and day out.

The private sector has experienced mixed fortunes in this new era, with private investment picking up on the back of liberalization and increased business confidence. Growth is still in capital-intensive rather than labour-intensive activity, and has remained well below the 5 per cent per annum that would be needed to dent unemployment. Businesspeople complain that profound skills deficiencies and labour market regulation militate against the employment growth the government seeks. Government is meanwhile looking to small and informal businesses, and perhaps public works, to create jobs. The devastation wrought by unemployment, however, is set to continue.

Black economic empowerment remains another priority given South Africa's history of racial division. Yet while empowerment will release entrepreneurial and intellectual energy in the longer term, it is costly now. ANC strategy has mostly steered a prudent course, balancing the costs of empowerment against the dangers of delay, and the ambition of Black entrepreneurs against the experience of their White peers. The challenge of HIV/AIDS casts a shadow over economy, society, and politics alike. The epidemic will burden managers and workers, increasing employee turnover and absenteeism, and reducing productivity. It will test the social fabric of the poorest communities and the political institutions of the new democracy. The epidemic is an exceptional challenge that requires a new level of co-operation between government, business and citizens, and better political leadership, if its worst potential implications are to be mitigated.

Reconciliation, Nation-building, and Democracy

Apartheid has left a residue of bitterness and suspicion. While some individuals transcended the segregation that blighted the twentieth century, generations will have to pass before race is no longer an impediment to trust. Policy makers have rightly given priority to reducing the profound inequalities of status and wealth that continue to stoke the fires of racial conflict. However equally taxing political challenges must soon be faced concerning the entrenchment of democracy and the establishment of an open and plural society.

On the surface democracy is South Africans' preferred form of rule. Open debate and political competition seem essential if conflicts of interest and opinion are to be accommodated. However, the language of democracy is complex and carries different meanings to different ears. Only a minority of (mostly White) beneficiaries of apartheid celebrate democracy for its promotion of political opposition and human rights (including the right to property). Most South Africans understand democracy primarily in instrumental terms, as a political form through which inequality is curtailed and basic public services, such as housing, water, and food, are made available to the people as a whole. The gulf between these interpretations of its meaning leaves South Africa's democracy vulnerable should economic injustice persist.

The ANC dominates the South African political landscape, and there are no challenges to its electoral power on the horizon. Indeed its strength helps to cushion fragile and awkward new institutions against the repercussions of conflict and inequality. South Africa's democracy is still too weak to cope with party fragmentation or racial polarization, because its lacks sound, legitimate, and trusted institutions. However, the longer the ANC continues unchallenged both electorally and in the executive, the more harm may be caused by state–party integration, patronage politics, opposition de-legitimation, and the abuse of incumbency.

Even the benefits of ANC dominance are far from assured. Its leadership sometimes places other former liberation movements above the rules of the democratic game, and privileges ANC mechanisms of accountability over the constitution. Can it be relied upon to bolster the legitimacy of the new political order? If this vast, sprawling, and ideologically diverse movement is unlikely to fall under the effective control of an authoritarian leadership, disenchanted activists may nevertheless abandon the ANC and voters might decide to stay at home. The brightest and best of the new generation are already turning their backs on politics and the public service. The ANC, if this continues, may progressively become the fiefdom of crude political entrepreneurs, the corrupt, and the cynically ambitious. An ANC weakened in this way would be unlikely to bring about a more equitable and benevolent distribution of the country's wealth and productive assets. Indeed, it might ultimately be responsible for a ruinous counter-reaction against entrenched injustice. This die is by no means cast. South Africa's plurality and political energy are already reasserting themselves. ANC leaders may succeed in sustaining their government as the engine of the country's social and economic transformation, and they might yet render the liberation movement a force for a more open and democratic politics.

Recommended Reading

1 Historical Context

There is a wealth of popular and academic writing on modern South African history. Excellent general histories include Beinart 2001, Worden 2000, Thompson 1990, Davenport 1991, and Saunders 2001. Sparks 1995 is a lively and stimulating journalistic survey of the negotiation process. On pre-twentieth-century history, see Beinart and Bundy 1987, Bundy 1988, and Wilson and Thompson 1982. On segregation and apartheid, see the collection of seminal essays in Beinart and Dubow 1995, and the contrasting viewpoints of Davies 1979, Wolpe 1988, and Lipton 1985. The internal strains of the apartheid project are explored in Posel 1991, Price 1991, and Greenberg 1987, and its black politics in Lodge 1985 and in the four volumes of Karis and Carter 1972–97. The demise of apartheid is analysed in Etherington 1994 and Stedman 1994. For elegant studies of the emergence of the Witwatersrand see Van Onselen 1982a and 1982b, and for a magical account of a twentieth century sharecropper see Van Onselen 1996.

2 A Rainbow Nation

On climate, ecology, and geography see Preston-Whyte and Tyson 1989, Morrell 2000, Haldenwang 1997, and Fox and Rowntree 2000. The meanings and significance of 'tribalism' and ethnicity in Southern Africa are explored in Bekker 1993, Mare 1992 and most illuminatingly Vail 1989. On Coloured and Indian South Africans, see Du Pre 1994, James and Simons 1989, Desai 1997, and Freund 1995.

3 The South African Economy

For orthodox overviews of macro-economic policy challenges, see Nattrass 1992 and 2000, and for a leftist perspective see Marais 1999. Developmental challenges are explored in May 2000 and Coetzee *et al.* 2001, and transition policy issues in Mitchie and Padayachee 1997. For a variety of views on black economic empowerment and affirmative action, see Qunta 1995, Adam *et al.* 1997, Idasa 1995, and Ramphele 1995. General business information can be found in McGregor's 1999. On labour relations, see Nel 1997.

4 Social Structure and Social Policy

Class, social structure, and employment are explored in Seekings and Nattrass forthcoming and Crankshaw 1996. For social welfare, see Taylor 2002 and

DSD 2001. For electrification see DME 1998, and for water and sanitation Skinner and Mqadi 1999, Hemson 2000, and Schmitz 1999. Critical analysis of housing, urban social infrastructure, and privatization policy can be found in Smith 2000, Bond 2000, and Makgetla 2001. For household survey evidence see Statistics South Africa 2001 and 2002c.

5   Government

Venter 2001 offers a readable guide to government and politics in South Africa. On intergovernmental relations, see Levy and Tapscott 2001b, Murray 2001, Ajam 2001, and Levy 2001. For discussion of the role of local government, see Parnell *et al.* 2002, and Cameron 1999 and 2000. On the structure of the Presidency see Jacobs 2000 and Presidency 2000.

6   Political Life

On the evolution of post-1994 politics, Lodge 1999 and 2002, and Schrire 2001 are essential. A more gloomy view is advanced in Giliomee and Simkins 1999. For briefer overviews see Mattes 2002 and Butler 2003

7   Culture, Ideas, and Issues

For a fascinating overview of South Africa's post-1994 culture see Kriger and Zegeye 2001 (upon which Chapter 7 drew heavily). On music see Erlmann 1999, and on religion Chidester 1992. For investigation of emerging lifestyles and consumption patterns see Burgess 2002. Issues in intercultural dialogue are explored illuminatingly in Kaschula and Anthonissen 1995. Steinberg 2001 offers an eye-opening introduction to crime and policing in South Africa.

8   South Africa and the World

For historical overviews see Barber and Barrett 1990, Geldenhuys 1990, and Olivier and Geldenhuys 1996. On the security state and the military, see Seegers 1996, Alden 1995, Hanlon 1986, and Grundy 1986. Exile diplomacy is detailed in Thomas 1996 and contemporary developments can he followed in SAIIA 2002 (annual).

South Africa on the Internet

South African Government Online <www.gov.za> offers an overview of the system of government, ministers' speeches, policy documents and statements, and links to political parties, government departments and agencies. The most useful official sources are the Treasury <www.Treasury.gov.za> and the national statistics agency <www.statssa.gov.za>. Current policy analysis is available from <www.polity.org.za>, which also contains useful commentaries. The National Economic Development and Labour Council <www.nedlac.org.za> provides insight into government–labour–business relations. Key political party sites include the ANC <www.anc.org.za> and its labour and communist allies <www.cosatu.org.za> and <www.sacp.org.za>. The official opposition Democratic Alliance can be found at <www.da.org.za>.

Non-governmental organizations can be accessed through the South African NGO network at <www.sangonet.org.za>. Useful and informative NGO sites include Institute for Democracy in South Africa <www.idasa.org.za>, Electoral Institute of South Africa <www.eisa.org.za>, and the business-sponsored Centre for Development and Enterprise <www.cde.org.za>. The best independent policy research is conducted by Centre for Policy Studies <www.cps.org.za>. Important development-related sites include Development Bank of Southern Africa <www.dbsa.org.za> and international organizations the World Bank and United Nations Development Programme <www.worldbank.org> and <www.undp.org>.

For information and analysis on HIV/AIDS, see international sites <www.unaids.org> and <www.aegis.com> (which has an excellent search facility). The University of Natal's Health Economics and HIV/AIDS Research Division <www.und.ac.za/und/heard/> has AIDS sectoral briefings, and campaign group Treatment Action Campaign <www.tac.org.za> has analysis and links. Projections of the impact of HIV/AIDS can be found on the Actuarial Society of South Africa site at <www.assa.org.za>.

Useful media sites include pre-eminent business newspaper Business Day <www.bday.co.za> and online Daily Mail and Guardian <www.mg.co.za> which has a searchable archive. The universities of Cape Town <www.uct.ac.za>, Witwatersrand <www.wits.ac.za>, and Stellenbosch <www.sun.ac.za> all have interesting sites and links. For international relations, see the official sites of the New Partnership for Africa's Development <www.nepad.org>, and the African Union <www.africa-union.org>. All listed sites were accessible 1 May 2003.

Bibliography

Adam, H., F. Van Zyl Slabbert, and K. Moodley (1997), *Comrades in Business* (Cape Town: Tafelberg).

Ajam, T. (2001), 'Intergovernmental fiscal relations', in Levy and Tapscott 2001a.

Alden, C. (1995), *Apartheid's Last Stand: The Rise and Fall of the South African Security State, 1978–90* (London: Macmillan).

Alexander, N. and K. Heugh (2001), 'Language policy in the New South Africa', in Kriger and Zegeye 2001.

Asmal, K. (1995), 'The making of a constitution', *Southern African Review of Books* No. 36.

ASSA (2002 and 2003), *Actuarial Society of South Africa AIDS Model* (Cape Town: Actuarial Society of South Africa) at <www.assa.org.za/aidsmodel.asp> [6 February 2003].

Barber, J. and J. Barratt (1990), *South Africa's Foreign Policy: The Search for Status and Security 1945–88* (Cambridge: Cambridge University Press).

Barber, J. and B. Vickers (2001), 'South Africa's foreign policy', in Venter 2001.

Beinart, W. (1994), *Twentieth Century South Africa* (Oxford: Oxford University Press).

Beinart, W. (2001), *Twentieth Century South Africa.* 2nd edn (Oxford: Oxford University Press).

Beinart, W. and C. Bundy (1987), *Hidden Struggles in Rural South Africa: The Politics and Popular Movements in the Transkei and Eastern Cape, 1890–1930* (Johannesburg: Ravan).

Beinart, W. and S. Dubow (1995) (eds), *Segregation and Apartheid in 20th Century South Africa* (London: Routledge).

Bekker, S. (1993), *Ethnicity in Focus: The South African Case* (Durban: Indicator South Africa).

Bhinda, N., S. Griffiths-Jones, J. Leape, and M. Martin (1999), *Private Capital Flows to Africa: Perception and Reality* (The Hague: FONDAD).

Bond, P. (2000), *Cities of Gold: Townships of Coal* (Trenton: Africa World Press).

Bonner, P., P. Delius, and D. Posel (1993) (eds), *Apartheid's Genesis 1935–1962* (Johannesburg: Witwatersrand University Press).

Bundy, C. (1988), *The Rise and Fall of the South Africa Peasantry*, 2nd edn (London: James Currey).

Burgess, S.M. (2002), *SA Tribes: Who We Are, How We Live and What We Want From Life in the New South Africa* (Cape Town: David Philip).

Butler, A. (2003), 'South Africa's political futures', *Government and Opposition* 38: 1.

Byrnes, R. (1997) (ed.), *South Africa: A Country Study* (Washington: Library of Congress).

Cameron, R. (1999), *The Democratisation of South African Local Government: A Tale of Three Cities* (Pretoria: van Schaik).

Cameron, R. (2000), 'Megacities in South Africa: A Solution for the New Millennium?' *Public Administration and Development* 20: 155–65.

Chidester, D. (1992), *Religions of South Africa* (London: Routledge).
Christopher, A.J. (2001). *The Atlas of Changing South Africa*. 2nd edn (London: Routledge).
Coetzee, J., J. Graaff, F. Hendricks, and G. Wood (2001) (eds), *Development: Theory, Policy and Practice* (Cape Town: Oxford University Press).
Cooper, F. (1996), *Decolonisation and African Society: The Labour Question in French and British Africa* (Cambridge: Cambridge University Press).
Crankshaw, O. (1997), *Race, Class and the Changing Division of Labour under Apartheid* (London: Routledge).
Crocker, C.R. (1992), *High Noon in Southern Africa: Making Peace in a Rough Neighbourhood* (New York: Norton).
Crush, J. and D.A. McDonald (2003) *Destinations Unknown* (Johannesburg: Africa Institute of South Africa).
Davenport, T.R.H. (1991), *South Africa: A Modern History*. 4th edn (London: Macmillan).
Davies, R. (1979), *Capital, State and White Labour in South Africa in 1900–1960: An Historical Materialist Analysis of Class Formation and Class Relations* (Brighton: Harvester).
Desai, A. (1997), *Arise ye Coolies: Apartheid and the Indian, 1960–1995* (Johannesburg: Impact Africa).
DFID (2001), *Meeting the Challenge of Poverty in Urban Areas* (London: UK Department for International Development).
DME (1998), *White Paper on the Energy Policy of the Republic of South Africa* (Pretoria: Department of Minerals and Energy Affairs).
DSD (2001), *The Road to Social Development* (Pretoria: Department for Social Development).
Du Pre, R.H. (1994), *Separate but Unequal: The 'Coloured' People of South Africa* (Johannesburg: Ball).
Erlmann, V. (1999), *Music, Modernity and the Global Imagination: South Africa and the West* (Oxford: Oxford University Press).
Etherington, N. (1994), 'Is it too early to start devising historical explanations for the end of apartheid?', in Rich 1994.
Fine, B. and Z. Rustomjee (1996), *Political Economy of South Africa* (Johannesburg: Witwatersrand University Press).
Fleishman, M. (2001), 'Unspeaking the centre', in Krige and Zegeye 2001.
Forrest D. and B. Streek (2001), 'Mbeki in bizarre AIDS outburst', *Weekly Mail and Guardian*, 26 October, archive availability <www.mg.co.za>.
Fourie, P. and M. Schonteich (2001), 'Africa's new security threat', *African Security Review* 10: 4.
Fox R. and K. Rowntree (2000) (eds), *Geography of South Africa in a Changing World* (Cape Town: Oxford University Press).
Freund, W. (1995), *Insiders and Outsiders* (London: James Currey).
GCIS (2002), *South African Yearbook 2001/2* (Pretoria: Government Communications and Information Service).
Geldenhuys, D. (1990) *Isolated States: A Comparative Analysis* (Johannesburg: Ball).
Giliomee, H. and C. Simkins (1999) (eds), *The Awkward Embrace: One-party Domination and Democracy* (Cape Town: Tafelberg).

Goodman, J.B. and L.W. Pauly (1993), 'The obsolescence of capital controls? Economic management in an age of global markets', *World Politics* 46: 50–82.

Greenberg, S.B. (1980), *Race and State in Capitalist Development* (Johannesburg: Ravan).

Greenberg, S.B. (1987), *Legitimating the Illegitimate: State, Markets, and Resistance in South Africa* (Berkeley: University of California).

Grint, K. (2000), *The Arts of Leadership* (Oxford: Oxford University Press).

Grundy, K.W. (1986), *The Militarization of South African Politics* (Bloomington: University of Indiana Press).

Haldenwang, B. (1997), *A Socio-demographic Profile of the South African Development Community Region* (Stellenbosch: University of Stellenbosch Institute for Futures Research).

Hanlon, J. (1986), *Apartheid's Second Front* (London: Penguin).

Hemson, D. (2000), 'Policy and practice in water and sanitation', *Indicator South Africa* 17(4): 48–53

Idasa (1995), *Making Affirmative Action Work* (Cape Town: Institute for Democracy in South Africa).

Idasa (2002a), 'Democratic governance in South Africa: the people's view', *Afrobarometer* 11 December 2002 archived at <www.idasa.org.za> [7 February 2003].

Idasa (2002b), 'The changing public agenda', *Afrobarometer* 11 December archived at <www.idasa.org.za> [7 February 2003].

Idasa (2002c), 'Political party support in South Africa', *Afrobarometer* 13 December archived at <www.idasa.org.za> [7 February 2003].

Impey, A. (2001), 'Re-fashioning identity in post-apartheid South African music', in Kriger and Zegeye 2001.

Jacobs, S. (2000), 'An imperial presidency?', *SAIRR Regional Topic Paper* (Johannesburg: South African Institute for Race Relations).

James, W.G. and M. Simons (1989) (eds), *The Angry Divide* (Cape Town: David Philip).

Johnson, R.W. and L. Schlemmer (1996), *Launching Democracy in South Africa* (New Haven: Yale University Press).

Johnston, A. (1994), 'South Africa: the election and the emerging party system', *International Affairs* 70(4): 721–36.

Karis, T. and G.M. Carter (1972–77), *From Protest to Challenge: A Documentary History of African Politics in South Africa 1882–1964*, 4 volumes (Stanford: Hoover Institution Press).

Kaschula, R. and C. Anthonissen (1995), *Communicating Across Cultures in South Africa* (Johannesburg: Hodder and Stoughton).

Kriger, R. and A. Zegeye (2001), *Culture in the New South Africa* (Cape Town: Kwela Books).

Lomon, A. (1991) (ed.), *Homes Apart* (Cape Town: David Philip).

Levy, N. (2001), 'Instruments of intergovernmental relations', in Levy and Tapscott 2001a.

Levy, N. and C. Tapscott (2001a) (eds), *Intergovernmental Relations in South Africa* (Cape Town: IDASA).

Levy, N. and C. Tapscott (2001b), 'Intergovernmental relations in South Africa', in Levy and Tapscott 2001a.

Lipton, M. (1985), *Capitalism and Apartheid: South Africa, 1910–84* (Aldershot: Gower).

Lodge, T. (1985), *Black Politics in South Africa since 1945* (London: Longman).
Lodge, T. (1999), *Consolidating Democracy: South Africa's Second Popular Election* (Johannesburg: Witwatersrand University Press).
Lodge, T. (2002), *Politics in South Africa: From Mandela to Mbeki* 2nd edn (Oxford: James Currey).
Lonsdale, J. (1988) (ed.), *South Africa in Question* (Cambridge: Cambridge University Press).
MacDonald, M. (1992), 'The siren's song: The political logic of power-sharing in South Africa', *Journal of Southern African Studies* 18(4): 709–25.
Makgetla N. (2001), 'Policies and realities: the state of privatisation', *South African Labour Bulletin* 25(4): 16–23.
Mahdi, P.M. (1997), *Black Economic Empowerment in the New South Africa* (Randburg: Knowledge Resources).
Mamdani, M. (1996), *Citizen and Subject: Contemporary Africa and the Legacy of Late Colonialism* (Princeton: Princeton University Press).
Mandela, N. (1993), 'South Africa's future foreign policy', *Foreign Affairs* 72(5): 86–97.
Marais, H. (1999), *South Africa: Limits to Change* (Cape Town: University of Cape Town Press).
Mare, G. (1992), *Brothers Born of Warrior Blood: Politics and Ethnicity in South Africa* (Johannesburg: Ravan).
Mattes, R. (1995), *The Election Book* (Cape Town: IDASA).
Mattes, R. (2002), 'South Africa: democracy without the people', *Journal of Democracy* 13(1): 22–36.
May, J. (2000) (ed.), *Poverty and Inequality in South Africa* (Cape Town: David Philip).
McGregor, R. (1999), *McGregor's Who Owns Whom in South Africa* (Johannesburg: Purdey Publishing).
Mitchie, J. and V. Padayachee (1997) (eds), *Political Economy of South Africa's Transition: Policy Perspectives in the Late 1990s* (London: Dryden Press).
Mokaba P. *et al.* (2002), *Castro Hlongwane, Caravans, Cats, Geese, Foot and Mouth and Statistics: HIV/AIDS and the struggle for the humanisation of the African* (unpublished unofficial discussion document) available at <www.chico.mweb.co.za/doc/aid.Castro.Hlongwane.doc> [20/09/2002]
Moll, T. (1990) 'From booster to brake: apartheid and economic growth in comparative perspective', in Nattrass and Ardington 1990.
Morrell, R. (2000) (ed.), *Changing Man in Southern Africa* (Pietermaritzberg: University of Natal Press).
Muradzikwa, S. (2002), *Foreign Investment in SADC* (University of Cape Town: Development Policy Research Unit, working paper 02/67).
Murray, C. (2001), 'Constitutional context of intergovernmental relations in South Africa', in Levy and Tapscott 2001a.
National Treasury (2002), *Budget Review 2002* (Pretoria: South African National Treasury).
Nattrass, N. and E. Ardington (1990) (eds), *Political Economy of South Africa* (Cape Town: Oxford University Press).
Nattrass, N. (1992), *Profits and Wages: The South African Economic Challenge* (Johannesburg: Penguin).
Nattrass, N. (2000), *Macroeconomics: Theory and Policy in South Africa* (Cape Town: David Philip).

Nattrass, N. and J. Seekings (2001), '"Two Nations"? Race and economic inequality in South Africa today,' *Daedalus* 130(1): 45–70.

Nel, P.S. (1997) (ed.), *South African Industrial Relations* (Pretoria: Van Schaik).

Olivier, G. and D. Geldenhuys (1997), 'South Africa's foreign policy: from idealism to pragmatism', *Business and the Contemporary World* 9(2).

Parnell, S., E. Pieterse, M. Swilling, and D. Wooldridge (2002) (eds), *Democratising Local Government: The South African experiment* (Cape Town: University of Cape Town Press).

Posel, D. (1991), *The Making of Apartheid* (Oxford: Clarendon).

Presidency (2000), *Integrated Democratic Governance: A Restructured Presidency at Work* (Pretoria: Presidency of the Republic of South Africa Communications Research Unit).

Preston-Whyte, R. and P. Tyson (1989), *Atmosphere and Weather of Southern Africa* (Cape Town: Oxford University Press).

Price, R. (1991), *The Apartheid State in Crisis: Political Transformation in South Africa, 1975–1990* (Oxford: Oxford University Press).

Qunta, C. (1995), *Who's Afraid of Affirmative Action* (Cape Town: Kwela).

Ramphele, M. (1995), *The Affirmative Action Book* (Cape Town: IDASA).

Rape Crisis Cape Town (2002), 'Statistics', available at <www.rapecrisis.org.za> [01/05/2003].

Reddy, T. (2002), 'The dominant party and democratic control', unpublished paper presented to the Department of Political Studies, University of Cape Town, 23 April 2002.

Rich P.B. (1994) (ed.), *The Dynamics of Change in Southern Africa* (London: Macmillan).

RSA (1995), *Labour Relations Act* (Pretoria: Republic of South Africa; Act No. 66 of 1995).

RSA (1996), *Constitution of the Republic of South Africa* (Pretoria: Republic of South Africa; Act No. 108 of 1996).

RSA (1997), *Basic Conditions of Employment Act* (Pretoria: Republic of South Africa; Act No. 75 of 1997).

RSA (1998a), *Employment Equity Act* (Pretoria: Republic of South Africa; Act No. 55 of 1998).

RSA (1998b), *Competition Act* (Pretoria: Republic of South Africa; Act No. 89 of 1998).

RSA (2002), *Mineral and Petroleum Resources Development Act* (Pretoria: Republic of South Africa; Act No. 28 of 2002).

Sadie, Y. (2001), 'Political parties and interest groups', in Venter 2001.

SAIIA (2002), *Yearbook of International Affairs* (Johannesburg: South African Institute for International Affairs, annual).

Saunders, C. (2001), *A Dictionary of South African History* 2nd edn (Cape Town. David Philip).

Schmitz, T. (1999), 'Rethinking delivery? A review of the efforts of the Department of Water Affairs, 1994–9', *Centre for Social Studies Policy Brief No. 16* (Johannesburg: Centre for Policy Studies).

Schrire, R. (2001), 'Realities of opposition in South Africa', *Democratization* 8(1).

Schrire, R. (1994) (ed.), *Malan to de Klerk: Leadership in the Apartheid State* (London: Hurst).

Seegers, A. (1996), *The Military in the Making of Modern South Africa* (London: Taurus).

Seekings, J. (1993), *Heroes or Villains? Youth Politics in the 1980s* (Johannesburg: Ravan).

Seekings, J. and N. Nattrass (forthcoming), *From Race to Class: Inequality, Unemployment and the Social Structure in South Africa* (Yale University Press).

Sisk, T. (1995), *Democratization in South Africa* (Princeton: Princeton University Press).

Skinner, K. and N. Mqadi (1999), 'Women and water', *Indicator South Africa* 16(2).

Smaldone, J. (1997), 'National security', in Byrnes 1997.

Smith, D. (2000) (ed.), *The Apartheid City and Beyond* (London: Routledge).

Southall, R. (2001), 'Conclusions', in *Democratization* 8(1).

Sparks, A. (1995), *Tomorrow is Another Country* (New York: Hill and Wang).

Stadler, A. (1987), *The Political Economy of Modern South Africa* (London: Croom Helm).

Statistics South Africa (2001), *South Africa in Transition: Selected Findings From the October Household Survey of 1999 and Changes That Have Occurred Between 1995 and 1999* (Pretoria: Statistics South Africa).

Statistics South Africa (2002a), *Statistics in Brief 2002* (Pretoria: Statistics South Africa).

Statistics South Africa (2002b), *Earning and Spending in South Africa* (Pretoria: Statistics South Africa).

Stedman, S.J. (1994) (ed.), *South Africa: The Political Economy of Transformation* (London: Lynne Rienner).

Steinberg, J. (2001) (ed.), *Crimewave* (Johannesburg: Witwatersrand University Press).

Taylor, V. (2002) (chairperson), *Transforming the Present – Protecting the Future: Report of the Committee of Inquiry into a Comprehensive System of Social Security for South Africa* (Pretoria: Department of Social Development).

Taylor, R. and M. Orkin (1995), 'The racialisation of social scientific research on South Africa', *South African Sociological Review* 7(2): 43–69.

Teer-Tomaselli, R. (2001), 'Nation-building, social identity and television in a changing media landscape', in Kriger and Zegeye 2001.

Thomas, S. (1996), *Diplomacy of Liberation* (Johannesburg: Taurus).

Thompson, L. (1990), *A History of South Africa* (London: Yale University Press).

UNCTAD (1999), *Foreign Direct Investment in Africa: Performance and Potential* (New York and Geneva: United National Conference on Trade and Development).

UNDP (2002), *Human Development Report 2002: Deepening democracy in a fragmented world* (Oxford: Oxford University Press and the United Nations Development Program).

Vail, L. (1989) (ed.), *Creation of Tribalism in Southern Africa* (London: James Currey).

Van Onselen, C. (1982a), *Studies in the Social and Economic History of the Witwatersrand 1886–1914: Volume I New Babylon* (Johannesburg: Ravan).

Van Onselen, C. (1982b), *Studies in the Social and Economic History of the Witwatersrand 1886–1914: Volume II New Ninevah* (Johannesburg: Ravan).

Van Onselen, C. (1996), *The Seed is Mine* (Cape Town: David Philip).

Venter, A. (2001) (ed.), *Government and Politics in the New South Africa* (Pretoria: Van Schaik).

Wilson, M. and L. Thompson (1982) (eds), *A History of South Africa to 1870*, 2nd edn (London: James Currey).

Wolpe, H. (1988), *Race, Class and the Apartheid State* (London: James Currey).

Worden, N. (1994), *The Making of Modern South Africa: Conquest, Segregation and Apartheid* (Oxford: Blackwell).

Worden, N. (2000), *The Making of Modern South Africa: Conquest, Segregation and Apartheid* 3rd edn (Oxford: Blackwell).

Yashar, D. (1997), *Demanding Democracy: Reform and Reaction in Costa Rica and Guatemala, 1870s–1950s* (Stanford: Stanford University Press).

Index